ACROSS
GREENLAND'S
ICE CAP

Alfred de Quervain in Greenland, 1909.

ACROSS GREENLAND'S ICE CAP

ALFRED DE QUERVAIN

The Remarkable Swiss Scientific Expedition of 1912

McGill-Queen's University Press
Montreal & Kingston • London • Chicago

ISBN 978-0-2280-1066-1 (cloth)
ISBN 978-0-2280-1266-5 (ePDF)

Legal deposit second quarter 2022
Bibliothèque nationale du Québec

Printed in Canada on acid-free paper

Published with the support of the Swiss Polar Institute and the Swiss Committee on Polar and High Altitude Research of the Swiss Academies of Arts and Sciences.

Library and Archives Canada Cataloguing in Publication
Title: Across Greenland's ice cap : the remarkable Swiss scientific expedition of 1912 / Alfred de Quervain.
Other titles: Quer durchs Grönlandeis. English
Names: Quervain, Alfred de, 1879-1927, author.
Description: Translation of: Quer durchs Grönlandeis: Die Expeditionen 1909 und 1912/13. | Includes bibliographical references and index.
Identifiers: Canadiana (print) 20210395060 | Canadiana (ebook) 2021039515X | ISBN 9780228010661 (cloth) | ISBN 9780228012665 (ePDF)
Subjects: LCSH: Quervain, Alfred de, 1879-1927—Travel—Greenland. | LCSH: Schweizerische Grönland-Expedition (1912-1913) | LCSH: Scientific expeditions—Greenland. | LCSH: Greenland—Discovery and exploration. | LCSH: Arctic regions—Discovery and exploration.
Classification: LCC G743 .Q813 2022 | DDC 919.8/204—dc23

This book is dedicated to the memory of Konrad Steffen (1952–2020)

Like Alfred de Quervain, Konrad Steffen was a pioneer of Swiss polar research. The coloured photographs of de Quervain's expedition, as published here, document a voyage through space, giving us a first glimpse of Greenland's cold, harsh beauty. For his part, Koni travelled through time on the Greenland ice sheet by researching its secrets for more than thirty years. His work opened the eyes of the world to the ice cap's vulnerability. Swiss Camp, the year-round monitoring station established by Koni, was located on the ice sheet near Ilulissat, from where de Quervain started his expedition in 1912. The data collected there afforded new insights into the physics of the ice sheets and the water flow in their deep interior. In recent decades, the measurements increasingly reflected the ice sheet's accelerated melting due to global heating. Koni raised an authentic and persuasive voice of warning against the dramatic environmental changes for which human activity is responsible. First and foremost, he was a dedicated scientist and a generous leader, a dear colleague and friend, whom we tragically lost on the Greenland ice cap.

Thomas Stocker
Professor of Climate and Environmental Physics, University of Bern

CONTENTS

PREFACE TO THIS EDITION

MARTIN HOOD

The year 1912 came in as a grand culmination of the heroic age of polar exploration. In January, a triumphant Roald Amundsen returned to his ship after attaining the South Pole. Just weeks later, Wilhelm Filchner had a narrow escape when his camp drifted out into the Weddell Sea on an errant iceberg.

In March, returning from the South Pole, Captain Scott and his companions reached the camp that would become their last resting place. That same month, all unaware of this tragedy and with minimal experience of polar travel, four young men left Zurich by train, fired with the ambition of making the first west-to-east crossing of Greenland's ice cap.

Few outside Switzerland have heard of this expedition or its leader, the meteorologist Alfred de Quervain. One reason was its very success. In just thirty-one days, the party crossed 640 kilometres of untracked snow and ice. Nobody died, fell into a crevasse, or suffered frostbite.

They didn't even run short of food, unlike Fridtjof Nansen's party during the first crossing of Greenland back in 1888. And while Nansen, travelling from east to west, had to take a shorter, more southerly line than planned, the Swiss expedition reached the opposite coast more or less on schedule.

Yet this was more than just a well-executed feat of Arctic adventure. On the way, de Quervain and his colleagues collected scientific data that, a century later, are more important than ever. Today's researchers still refer to the Swiss expedition's glacier survey and the height profile they made of the ice sheet while crossing it.

Like today's expeditioners, de Quervain struggled to pay off the expedition's debts. Some of the money came from subsequent lecture tours around Switzerland, showing hand-tinted lantern slides. (A selection of these illustrations appear in this book.) He was also quick to write up a popular account of his adventures, publishing it in 1914 as *Quer durchs Grönlandeis: Die Schweizerische Grönland-Expedition 1912/13*.

Long after de Quervain's early death, his book was translated in the early 1980s by his daughter, Elisabeth de Quervain Schriever, and her husband, William, who had settled in Canada. As they explain in their original foreword (included this edition) to the unpublished manuscript, the Schrievers wanted to give their three children "a glimpse of a moment in the life of your grandfather."

It is this translation that we present here, in time to mark the 110th anniversary of de Quervain's expedition. The translation includes the two additional chapters that appeared in the 1914 edition. These were contributed by the scientists Paul-Louis Mercanton and August Stolberg, who remained on Greenland's west coast to research its glaciers and meteorology while de Quervain's quartet crossed the ice cap.

For this new edition, we have added an introduction outlining how de Quervain came to plan and execute his Greenland crossing. Glaciologists Andreas Vieli and Martin Lüthi of the University of Zurich weigh up the expedition's scientific results and explain why they remain significant to this day.

We hope this book will give you a glimpse of a remarkable adventure in science.

ACKNOWLEDGMENTS

Appropriately, work on this latest edition of Alfred de Quervain's book started during *Greenland 1912*, an exhibition at the Swiss National Museum in Zurich. Geoff Spearing, who worked on the exhibition's literature, let me know of Elisabeth and William Schriever's unpublished translation of de Quervain's 1914 text. This draft, kindly made available by the exhibition organizer, Dario Donati, has been a pleasure to edit; any remaining errors or omissions are the responsibility of the editor – namely, myself.

Then followed a pleasant supper with Daniel Meili, a grandson of Alfred de Quervain, who gave the family's blessing for this book project. Without Daniel's support and encouragement, and that of the other descendant families, this book could never have been published.

The same is true of Heike Hartmann of the ETH-Bildarchiv, part of the Swiss Federal Institute of Technology's library, and her colleagues, who left no effort unspared to locate, organize, and refine the image files from the original hand-tinted photographs for this edition. The book then found the ideal publisher, in the person of Richard Baggaley of McGill-Queen's University Press. Both the book's text and its selection of images have benefited immensely from his enthusiasm and judgment. I would also like to thank Maureen Garvie, whose unobtrusive yet expert copyediting lent wings to the flow of the text, and managing editor Kathleen Fraser, whose time discipline and high standards in producing this book matched those of the Swiss expeditioners themselves.

The book's introduction owes much to the pioneering work by William Barr, professor emeritus of the University of Saskatchewan, who was the first to present the 1912 expedition's achievements to the English-speaking world.[1]

Invaluable for setting matters in a wider cultural context was Lea Pfäffli's paper on Swiss scientific research in Greenland during the run-up to the First World War.[2] Key additional details for the introduction came from an appreciation of de Quervain's scientific career by Stefan Kern of the University of Hamburg.[3]

Meanwhile, Stephan Orth, grandson of expedition member Roderich Fick, provided a fresh and lively point of view in *Opas Eisberg* (Grandpa's Iceberg), published in 2015. The book is based on Fick's journal and Stephan Orth's own visits to Greenland to trace the expedition's route.[4]

We are also most grateful for an assessment of the expedition's scientific results to the glaciologists Andreas Vieli and Martin Lüthi of the University of Zurich, whose researches have built on the 1912 western party's survey of the Eqip Sermia glacier.

The expedition's legacy includes its trove of hand-coloured glass lantern slides. That we have been able to publish such a broad selection here is due to a generous subvention from the Swiss Polar Institute, the interdisciplinary body established in 2016 to coordinate the country's research programs in the Arctic and Antarctic regions, and the Swiss Committee on Polar and High Altitude Research (SKPH) of the Swiss Academies of Arts and Sciences.

As the researchers working with the SKPH and the Swiss Polar Institute are the true heirs of the scientific traditions established by de Quervain, their support has been particularly meaningful for all involved in the book's production. We would particularly like to thank Basil Fahrlaender and Christoph Kull for their unfailing encouragement for this project.

Martin Hood, Academic Alpine Club of Zurich
Zurich and Oxford, 1 August 2021

NOTES

1 Barr, "Alfred de Quervain's Swiss Greenland expedition."

2 Pfäffli, "Das Wissen, das aus der Kälte kam."

3 Kern, "Alfred de Quervain."

4 Orth, *Opas Eisberg*.

INTRODUCTION

MARTIN HOOD

After sledging all day through snow squalls or the ice cap's glare, the four men would unwind in their tent by having "learned conversations on Mach, Kant, Hume, and Schopenhauer." Even at rest, the 1912 Swiss expedition to Greenland was "a serious undertaking."

Every morning, an hour or so was dedicated to science. Inside the tent, the leader would boil up his hypsometer, an accurate way of gauging their height above sea level. Outside, a tall colleague used a theodolite to measure slope angles, whistling as he worked, a habit that intensely irritated the expedition leader.[1] Between the sledges, the expedition doctor attended to the dogs.

Meanwhile, the expedition's youngest member was shooting the sun through a sextant. All their lives depended on his position-finding. If they didn't find a pre-placed supply depot on Greenland's sketchily mapped east coast, no one would ever hear of them again.

None of the four explorers could have suspected that, a century hence, scientists would still be relying on the precision of their measurements.

To explain how four young men from Zurich crossed Greenland in the summer of 1912 requires a backwards glance into the history of meteorology and how that nascent science shaped the life of the expedition's leader.[2]

In hindsight, what took Alfred de Quervain to Greenland was the stratosphere. Nobody yet suspected its existence when he was born on 15 June 1879, the son of a rural pastor, at Uebeschi, a small village about thirty kilometres south of Bern, Switzerland's capital. By the time he reached his early twenties, de Quervain would be helping to bring about its discovery.

After studying geophysics and meteorology in Bern, de Quervain went to Paris to help Léon Teisserenc de Bort investigate the upper atmosphere. This was in 1898, the year that the French meteorologist started sending up instruments under hydrogen-filled paper balloons of his own design. These soundings showed that air temperatures stopped falling at a point about eleven kilometres above the ground. This finding was later billed as "the most surprising discovery in the whole history of meteorology."[3]

For that reason, Teisserenc de Bort proceeded with caution. Before he felt able to confirm his results, he spent several years establishing how they varied in altitude with latitude and the seasons. Some of these observations would be made by de Quervain.

In late 1900, the twenty-two-year-old de Quervain was despatched to St Petersburg and Moscow. There he spent the winter sending weather balloons swaying up into the frigid night skies. On his return journey, the suitcase containing his results was stolen, but fortunately he was able to recover the precious notebooks, which were worthless to the thief.

Returning to Bern, de Quervain completed his doctorate in 1903. Building on his apprenticeship in Paris, his dissertation described how temperature boundaries tend to dome upwards in the winds flowing over the Alps.

This work led to a post in Strassburg, then a Germany city, under Hugo Hergesell, chairman of the International Commission for Scientific Aviation (the Internationale Kommission für wissenschaftliche Luftfahrt, founded in 1896). As secretary to this body, de Quervain helped to coordinate and standardize the launches of weather balloons worldwide. In 1905, he devised an improved theodolite for tracking them.

It was in Strassburg that de Quervain first met August Stolberg, a colleague at the International Commission. An expert photographer and aeronaut, Stolberg would twice accompany his Swiss friend to Greenland. Soon de Quervain qualified as a balloon pilot himself. Having taken his *habilitation*, a postdoctoral qualification, he returned to Switzerland in 1906 to serve as adjunct-director of the Swiss Central Meteorological Office, the forerunner of the country's present-day weather forecasting agency. He would stay in this post, supporting the agency's director, for the rest of his career.

Meanwhile, his mentors were continuing to send up pilot balloons in northern climes. Professor Hergesell launched them over the Arctic Ocean in 1906. The following year, Teisserenc de Bort embarked on a lengthy expedition to Kiruna in Lapland for the same purpose.[4] It was in 1908 that the French scientist coined the word "stratosphere" to describe the upper air above the tropopause, that remarkable temperature boundary.

PRELIMINARIES: 1909 EXPEDITION TO WEST GREENLAND

These projects must have renewed de Quervain's appetite for high latitudes. Going north to study the upper atmosphere made sense. The stratosphere dips lower in the far north, and if balloon soundings were conducted in Greenland, they would add to the knowledge of how winds circulate around the pole.

These arguments helped to convince potential sponsors. Funded in part by Count Ferdinand von Zeppelin, the founder of the eponymous airship company and a close confidant of Hugo Hergesell, de Quervain set off on his first expedition to Greenland in the spring of 1909. He was accompanied by August Stolberg and Ernst Bäbler, a botanist from Zurich. On the last part of their journey up the west coast, they travelled in the company of the Swiss geologist Arnold Heim.

Some weather balloons were duly launched from Godthaab on the island's southwest coast, filled with hydrogen from cylinders furnished by the Zeppelin works at Friedrichshafen.[5] More striking than the meteorology, though, was the travellers' first encounter with Greenland's original inhabitants. As de Quervain recorded, "Up there, what one finds most remarkable are the people … We Europeans speak of Greenlanders as if they were well-behaved children, but how they manage to live in those conditions is no child's play, and it's only natural that they see themselves as different ... and on journeys they feel responsible for us as one would for a non-adult."[6] Inspired by the native "kayakmen," de Quervain soon procured one of their "genial vessels" for himself and started practising in it. A more serious study of Inuit culture would have to wait, although Bäbler did collect some skulls from a grave site to take back to Zurich. The expedition then made its way further north to inspect a glacier previously surveyed by Erich von Drygalski in 1892–93.

The German geophysicist was not de Quervain's only inspiration. He had also equipped himself with two sledges, complete with sails, which he had ordered from Norway on the pattern established by Fridtjof Nansen for his pioneering traverse of Greenland's ice cap in 1888. However, Nansen had started and finished his traverse further south than planned, leaving the central reaches of the ice cap unexplored.

Since then, Robert Peary and other sledge parties had explored Greenland's fringes, but nobody had again ventured across the ice cap from coast to coast. Could the Swiss expedition complete what Nansen had left unfinished? The ambition was there. With Stolberg and Bäbler, de Quervain started out from a camp on the Sermilik Fjord north of Uummannaq on 9 July 1909, man-hauling the sledges as Nansen had done. Soon they found that they had underestimated the challenge.

So slow was their progress over the pitted and crevassed ice that, on 24 July, they decided that Stolberg would stay with the tent to make accurate altitude readings, while de Quervain and Bäbler would dash eastwards for one more day, unburdened by the sledges. In the event, the two men reached a height of 1,700 metres before reluctantly turning back: "One last time, we swept our gaze across the entire expanse of ice, lingering longest in the east. To have to turn back now that we had a clear path, when we felt so strong and enterprising, this was bitter, bitter. But we would return! Then we turned and skied through the evening and night."

The three expeditioners returned to the ice cap's edge on 1 August, the day on which the Swiss celebrate the founding of their confederation, and spent the next two weeks surveying and photographing the glacier studied by Drygalski. De Quervain's bid to follow in Nansen's ski tracks, albeit on a more northerly track, had lapsed into a mere reconnaissance. But the lessons would be absorbed.

Back in Switzerland, de Quervain took on responsibility for Switzerland's first permanent seismological observatory. This was sited at Degenried, on a hilltop above Zurich. He also continued to make balloon flights, often for scientific ends. In October 1910, he ascended from Schlieren, near Zurich – after filling the balloon with coal gas from the municipal gas works – and flew at up to 2,800 metres above the morning fog before landing near Olten. On board was the physicist Albert Gockel, who used the flight to investigate what would later be recognized as cosmic rays.

PREPARATIONS FOR THE 1912 EXPEDITION

The following year was even busier. De Quervain married Elisabeth Nil, a teacher from the French-speaking Jura region north of Bern. Meanwhile, preparations for his second expedition moved up a gear. This enterprise would be all-Swiss, at least in its funding. After a range of scientific institutions, commercial firms, and private individuals had chipped in, the *Neue Zürcher Zeitung* newspaper came up with ten thousand Swiss francs, about a third of the total costs.

Funding and time constraints meant that this would be a lightweight expedition. Especially for the traverse, a small party must suffice. First to be selected was Hans Hössli, a recently qualified doctor who had worked as an assistant to de Quervain's older brother Fritz, a surgeon working in Basel. Hössli's record as an expert alpinist and exponent of "guideless climbing" must also have recommended him.

Next to present himself was Roderich Fick, a German-born architect with many practical skills. Knocking on de Quervain's door, he glimpsed a slip of paper bidding him to "please keep your visit short." This brusqueness would set the tone for much of their future working relationship. And with Fick came his friend Karl Gaule, also of German nationality, who had studied engineering in Zurich. These four would make up the traverse team, the so-called eastern party.

In addition, a supporting group was signed up. This comprised de Quervain's companion from the 1909 expedition, August Stolberg, as well as Dr Paul-Louis Mercanton of Geneva, a glaciologist and meteorologist, and Dr Wilhelm Jost of Bern, a glaciologist and accomplished photographer.

After helping the traverse party ferry their supplies onto the ice cap, this "western party" would spend the summer on the west coast, studying its weather and glaciers. Mercanton and Jost would also overwinter at Morten Porsild's Arctic research station at Godhavn, to continue their weather observations through the Arctic night.

As in 1909, the expedition would travel on scheduled steamer services, chartering a ship only for the last stage of their approach. This would keep costs down. Moreover, the traverse party would avoid overwintering in Greenland, as Nansen had been forced to do. And this, in turn, meant travelling fast – with dogs pulling the sledges.

De Quervain was well aware that the dogs were a weak point in his planning. Nobody in his team knew how to drive them. To perfect this vital skill, he had budgeted an interval of just a few weeks on their way up Greenland's west coast. Morten Porsild dismissed this scheme out of hand: "What would be your reply be to a good citizen of Copenhagen if he told you he would be travelling to Switzerland to climb Mont Blanc without a guide and, for practice, ascending the Blocksberg [a minor eminence in Germany] en route? … forget about the dogs; after six weeks of training at Holsteinsborg (!!) you will achieve nothing but anguish and unnecessary stress."[7]

Steamer schedules and summer sea-ice conditions added to the risk. These dictated that the Swiss expedition, unlike Nansen's, would start on the west coast, with its string of settlements, and finish on the sparsely populated east coast. But before they could reach the island outpost of Angmagssalik (today's Tasiilaq) on the east coast, they would have to find a pre-placed depot containing extra food and their kayaks. And such maps as existed could not be trusted.

De Quervain later admitted that they'd taken great risks. "But, on the other hand," he wrote, "so exact were we in devising and working out our preparations that perhaps some interesting but avoidable situations did not occur. For such would have been sensational and not to the credit of a serious undertaking."

Thus, for example, he sent Fick and Gaule on a winter foray to the high Engadine Valley to test the tent and supply a written report on the results. As the

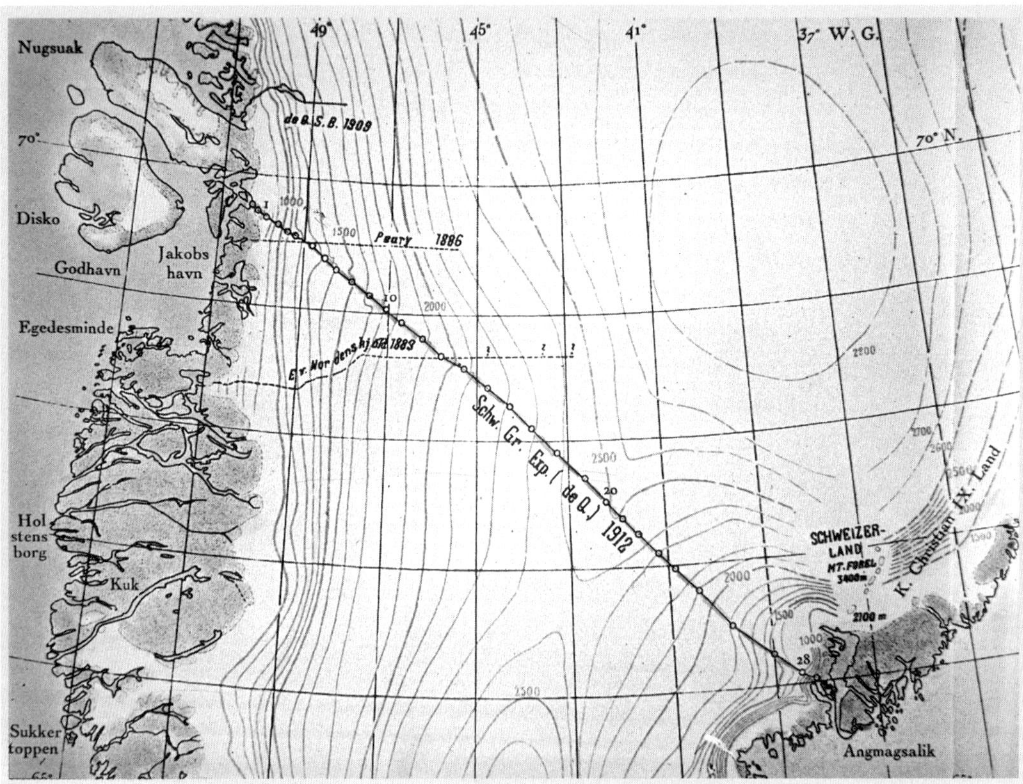

Figure 1

Map showing expanded view of the routes of the 1909 and 1912 expeditions.

Source: *Quer durchs Grönlandeis: Die Expeditionen 1909 und 1912/13.*

expedition's handyman, Fick also lit up a Nansen stove in his home workshop to find out how much fuel they would need, proved tent fabrics with a spring balance, and hand-built three kayaks. The first try at kayaking, on Lake Zurich, ended ignominiously when Gaule and Fick capsized.

The expeditioners left Zurich in late March 1912. In his diary, Roderich Fick recorded that, to reassure his family, he had likened the trip to spending half a year in military service, a duty that he'd already discharged in Germany. "But privately," he added, "I did have some fears or worries, as I thought our enterprise was rather hazardous."

There was reasonable cause for concern. Hardly any recent expedition to Greenland had escaped scot-free. Robert Peary had lost eight toes in 1899 on his third expedition, after breaking a leg on his second. Even fresher in memory was the Denmark expedition to Greenland's northeastern coast in 1906–08, from which its leader Ludvig Mylius-Erichsen and two companions had failed to return.

Taking ship in Copenhagen, the expedition reached Holstensborg in late April, leaving themselves less than a month to learn how to drive dogs. Progress was slow at first – the dogs' everyday savagery appalled the Swiss tyros, and learning how to wield a whip like a Greenlander hurt them more than it did the animals. And then de Quervain had a stroke of luck. His expedition doctor, Hans Hössli, turned out to have an aptitude for both dog handling and repairing the mission-critical sledge gear.

THE CROSSING

By 20 June, the expeditioners had hauled their sledges and supplies up to the ice cap. De Quervain felt himself at home: "Strange as it may seem, for me this cold ice felt neither sterile nor forbidding. It seemed quite familiar to me." A day or so later, the traverse party parted from their supporting group and headed into Greenland's unknown interior.

On 23 June, the expedition almost met its nemesis. Two of the three sledges, together with their dogs and drivers, crashed through the thin ice of a frozen lake. Only Hössli and the lead sledge escaped this "summer bath." Fortunately, the sleeping bags and the matches had been packed in waterproof bags or tins. One of the all-important chronometers was waterlogged, but de Quervain managed to get it running again.

After this near-disaster, the journey picked up pace. On the smoother snows of the interior, they started to exceed twenty kilometres day. And they settled

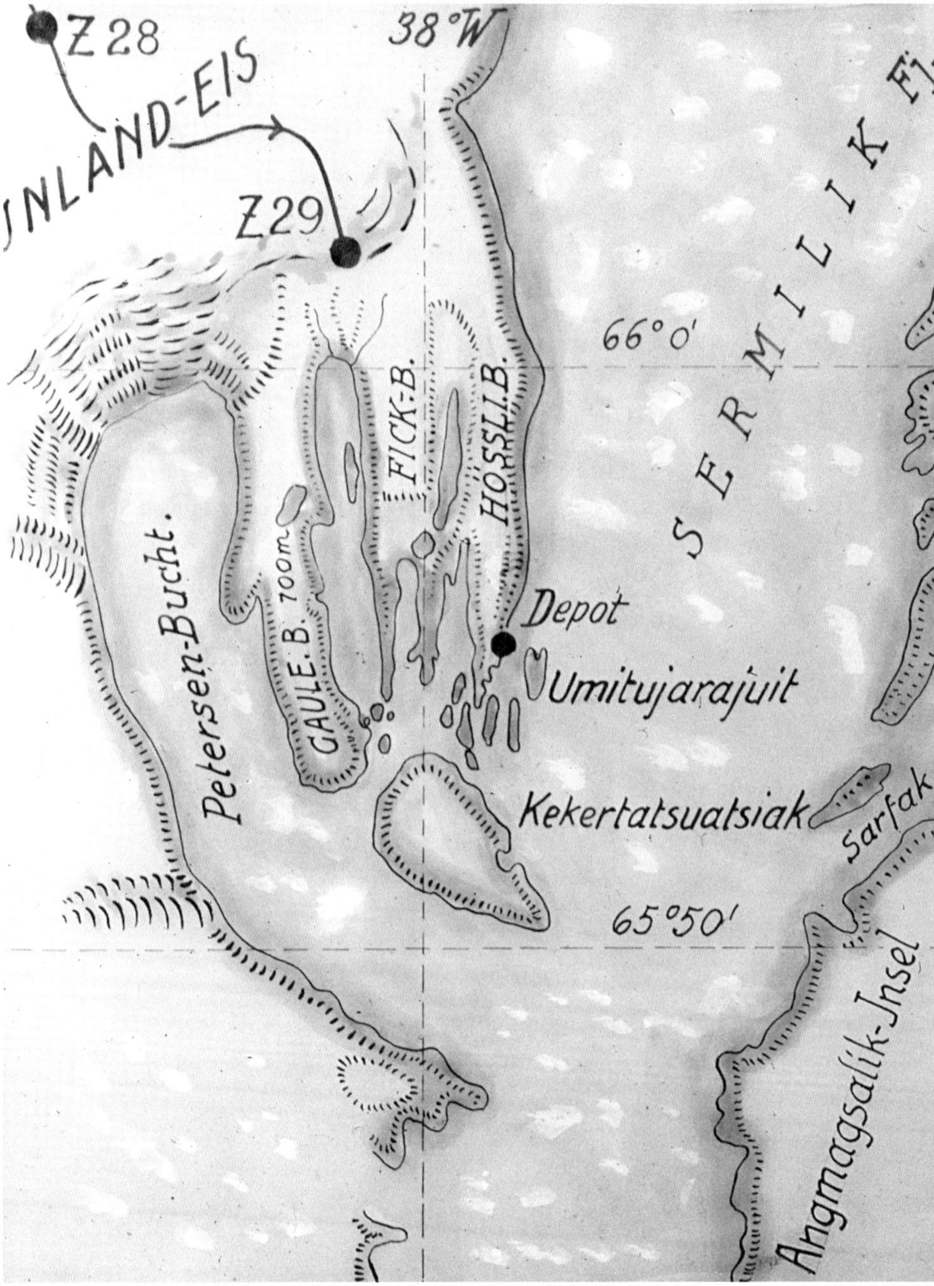

Figure 2

Sketch map of the depot's location on the east coast, 1912.

Source: de Quervain, *Quer durchs Grönlandeis: Die Expeditionen 1909 und 1912/13.*

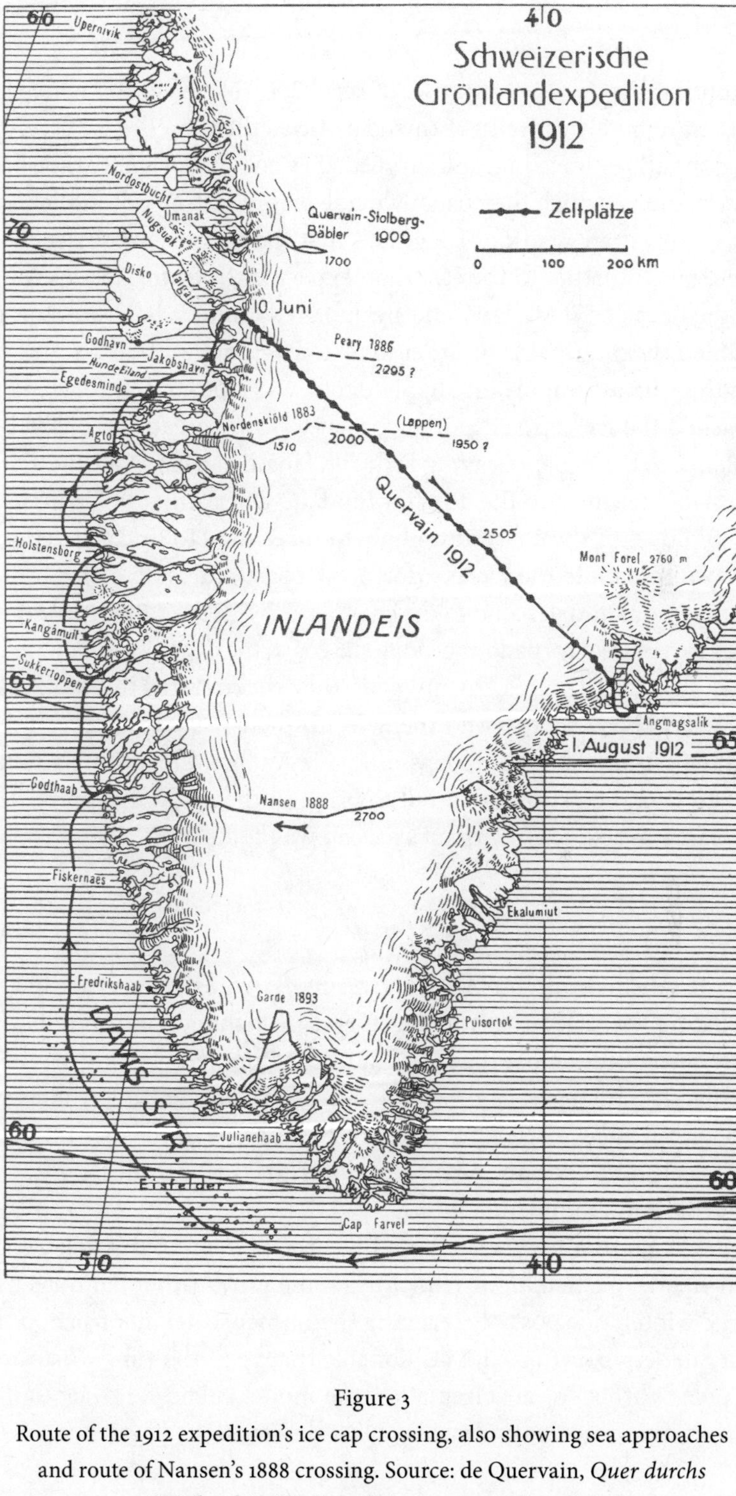

Figure 3
Route of the 1912 expedition's ice cap crossing, also showing sea approaches and route of Nansen's 1888 crossing. Source: de Quervain, *Quer durchs Grönlandeis: Die Expeditionen 1909 und 1912/13.*

into a routine. As de Quervain was to recollect, “Never in my whole life had I been even remotely as well-organized as I was there on the ice cap.” Having mastered the arts of travelling and survival, they could allow more time for scientific observations, which they usually made before setting out in the morning.

On 13 July, their readings suggested that they’d passed over the ice cap’s ridgeline, much further to the east than expected. In camp that evening, they ran up the flags of Switzerland and Bern on a sounding pole. And on 19 July, they sighted the mountains of the eastern coastal ranges.

Finding the all-important supply depot was not straightforward. When they reached the ice cap’s edge, the coastal terrain spread out below bore no resemblance to their map. Leaving Fick and Hössli at a campsite, with instructions to slaughter most of the dogs for food, de Quervain and Gaule set out to find a way down to the coast. It took them three days to find the depot, and a further two to paddle the kayaks down the coast and then climb back up to their companions and descend to the coast again with the full team and sledges.

After two more days paddling along the coast, the expeditioners were in their tent when they heard voices. Rushing out, they encountered three “kayakmen,” who may have been sent to find them. With their help, de Quervain himself reached the settlement of Angmagssalik on 1 August, the Swiss National Day. A few days later, boats were sent out to bring in the rest of his party. The first west-to-east traverse of Greenland’s ice cap was complete.

THE RECKONING

“We can be satisfied with our scientific results,” wrote de Quervain in October 1913. In listing the expedition’s achievements in chapter 12 of this book, he first cites the “new profile across the seven-hundred-kilometre breadth of the island of Greenland, the longest and most accurate to date,” with altitudes usually exact to within a few metres. In time, it would be one of the expedition’s most enduring legacies to science. The second part of this introduction weighs up that contribution in more detail.

At the time, though, it may have been the meteorologists who made the most impact. In particular, by launching some 120 weather balloons through the Arctic winter, one possibly reaching the immense height of 39,000 metres, Jost and Stolberg overturned a fashionable theory of the time. Instead of the stable “polar vortex” of air circulation the model called for, they found that wind directions varied considerably.

SEQUELS

Back in Switzerland, de Quervain and Hössli embarked on a busy program of public lectures illustrated with lantern slides. Their takings went to pay off the expedition's substantial debts. Probably for the same reason, de Quervain brought out his expedition book with admirable celerity.

Hans Hössli too was prompt in writing up his observations. An article in the 1913 yearbook of the Swiss Ski Association deals with polar expeditions and their equipment. The Swiss Army, he suggested, might do well to adopt the *kamik*, a soft Inuit boot for snow work. In 1914, he married Gertrud Haerle, also a doctor of medicine, and two children came along in the next few years. Hössli published a scholarly article in 1914 on the craniological measurements of Inuit skulls, building on studies he'd made at remote settlements in East Greenland. His academic excursions did no harm to Hössli's professional career. In 1917, still in his early thirties, he was appointed medical director of the Universitätsklinik Balgrist in Zurich, a top orthopaedic hospital. But just eight months later, the young doctor was dead, a victim of the 1918–19 influenza pandemic.

The expedition's youngest member, Karl Gaule, published little or nothing about his Greenland experiences. Instead, he took up a post at the Aeronautical Institute at Aachen's technical university as an assistant to Theodore von Kármán, who would later be known as a father of modern aerodynamics.

When the Great War broke out, Gaule joined a snowshoe battalion in the Carpathian Mountains, winning the Iron Cross before being repatriated to Germany. From mid-1915, he continued to apply his engineering skills to aircraft development and, latterly, water turbines, until his early death in 1922.

For his part, Roderich Fick went out to the German Cameroon in 1914 to head up the public works department. As an officer in the colony's defence forces, he was then interned by the Spanish authorities, first in Africa and then in Spain. Fick whiled away his captivity by working up his unpublished memoir of the Greenland expedition. These reminiscences inform *Opas Eisberg* (Grandpa's Iceberg), a book published in 2015 by Stephan Orth, Fick's descendant, who visited Greenland twice to trace his grandfather's footsteps.

After Hitler came to power, Fick's talents found favour with the regime and even with the Führer. A series of architectural commissions led up to his appointment as an advisor on a project to remodel the Austrian city of Linz where Hitler had spent his youth.

Ironically, the Linz assignment marked the start of Fick's fall from grace with the authorities. Even so, this association and his party membership were enough to earn him the postwar designation of "Mitläufer" (fellow traveller). Fick died in 1955, making him by far the longest-lived of the expeditioners.

THE LEGACY

After the expedition, Alfred de Quervain returned to his office at the Swiss Central Meteorological Office. He also continued to make balloon ascents. On occasion, these public and private activities flowed productively together.

In April 1913, for instance, a balloon lifted away from the playing field alongside Zurich's municipal gasworks. Accompanying de Quervain was the physicist Auguste Piccard, who was just then working towards his doctorate at the Federal Institute of Technology (ETH) in Zurich. As a balloonist in his own right, Piccard would later become the first aeronaut to reach the stratosphere.

The aeronauts carried with them an experiment on the balloon's gas temperatures, prepared with the help of Albert Einstein, then a recently appointed professor at the ETH and Piccard's supervisor.[8] But the apparatus was apparently not the main topic of conversation as the craft drifted southwards through the night. Instead, before landing the balloon at Buchs in the Rhine Valley, de Quervain and Piccard had roughed out the design for a new type of seismometer. To pick up weak subalpine earthquakes, they decided that the device would need a pendulum weighing more than twenty tonnes.

When installed at the Degenried observatory in 1922, this massive counterweight was assembled from shell case blanks loaned by the Swiss Army. A condition was attached: that, if war broke out, the metal blanks would be returned to the military authorities within forty-eight hours.

De Quervain also renewed his acquaintance with glaciers. In 1914, he surveyed the Claridenfirn glacier for the first time, initiating a series of measurements that would be repeated yearly up to the present day. Whether or not by coincidence, the spacious views of this gently sloping ice sheet in the Glarus Alps are curiously reminiscent of Arctic expanses.

Although de Quervain never returned to Greenland, a substitute locus for high-altitude research soon suggested itself. In the year he returned from the ice cap, the Jungfrau Railway was opened, after its engineers had spent more than a decade and a half blasting and tunnelling their way through the refractory limestone of the Eiger.

The project's founder and promoter, Adolf Guyer-Zeller, had always intended to support scientific endeavours at the Jungfraujoch but died before either the railway or a high-altitude observatory could be completed. It fell to de

Quervain to realize this vision. On his initiative, the Jungfraujoch Commission of the Schweizerische Naturforschende Gesellschaft (now the Swiss Academy of Sciences) was founded in 1922. This led to the construction of a temporary "meteorological pavilion" on the glacier four years later and to the opening of permanent research buildings during the 1930s.

These exertions may have hastened de Quervain's premature death. In 1924, he suffered a stroke after a working trip to the Jungfraujoch, which lies some three and a half kilometres above sea level. After making what seemed to be a complete recovery, he succumbed to a further stroke on 13 June 1927.

The brevity of de Quervain's life – he died at the age of just forty-seven – stands in contrast to the durability of his achievements. Atmospheric research is still conducted at the Jungfraujoch high-altitude observatory, and at Degenried you can still inspect the massive seismometer that was sketched out during a balloon flight. (It seems that the Swiss Army never did ask for the return of its shell blanks.)

Yet de Quervain's most lasting testament may lie in his scientific legacy, which is assessed in more detail below. His survey results from Greenland now provide a baseline for studies of the ice sheet's melting rate. And glaciologists from Zurich still survey the Claridenfirn every year, making this rapidly dwindling ice sheet the longest studied in the world. Recently, a lake of sky-blue water has formed at its snout, a sure sign that the days of this elegant and peaceful glacier are numbered.

NOTES

1 Stephan Orth, *Opas Eisberg: Auf Spurensuche durch Grönland* (Munich: Malik-National Geographic, 2015).

2 For a broad survey of de Quervain's career and Greenland expeditions, see William Barr, "Alfred de Quervain's Swiss Greenland Expeditions, 1909 and 1912," *Polar Record* 51, no. 4 (2015): 366–85.

3 The words are those of Sir Napier Shaw in his *Manual of Meteorology* (Cambridge: Cambridge University Press, 1926).

4 A. Rotch, "The Warm Stratum in the Atmosphere," *Nature* 78, no. 7 (1908).

5 Lea Pfäffli, "Das Wissen, das aus der Kälte kam: Assoziationen der Arktis um 1912," PhD diss., ETH Zürich, Diss ETH No. 26003 (2019).

6 Alfred de Quervain, *Quer durchs Grönlandeis: Die Expeditionen 1909 und 1912/13* (Zürich: Verlag Neue Zürcher Zeitung, 1998), 33.

7 Quoted in Barr, "Alfred de Quervain's Swiss Greenland Expedition," 370.

8 Stefan Kern, "Alfred de Quervain: Erforscher physikalischer Extreme und Überquerer des grönländischen Inlandeises," Polararchiv Schweiz blog, February 2017.

ALFRED DE QUERVAIN'S SCIENTIFIC LEGACY: AN APPRAISAL

ANDREAS VIELI and MARTIN LÜTHI

It is no coincidence that we chose the Eqip Sermia for our research project, the glacier where Alfred de Quervain started his crossing of the ice sheet. Our own aim, when we revisited this area between 2014 and 2018, was to investigate glacier calving over the long term, and the unique measurements from the Swiss 1912 expedition gave us exactly that: a long-term perspective. In addition, the very precise measurements made by our predecessors at the start of the expedition's route let us study the thickening and thinning of the ice sheet margin over the course of an entire century.

We have done fieldwork on a variety of glaciers and ice sheets during our scientific careers, but being able to tie our own research to de Quervain's legacy deepened our appreciation of his achievements. In what follows, we offer a scientific perspective on the 1912 expedition. Our viewpoint is naturally influenced by our research focus on glacier dynamics, and hence we do not pretend to cover all aspects of the expedition's research with equal depth.

Prior to de Quervain, exploration and discovery were the usual motives for polar expeditions. Science tended to come second, at least when it came to raising funds and seeking support from a wider public. It cannot be denied that de Quervain's ice cap crossing also had a whiff of adventure-seeking about it, yet scientific curiosity and research really did sit at the heart of this "serious undertaking," shaping every aspect of the planning and preparations.[1]

While crossing the ice sheet, the expedition's daily schedule was dictated by systematic scientific data-gathering such as geodetic surveys, meteorological observations, and the digging of snow profiles. And, as we have seen, the main task of the "western party," who stayed behind on the coast, was to survey the ice

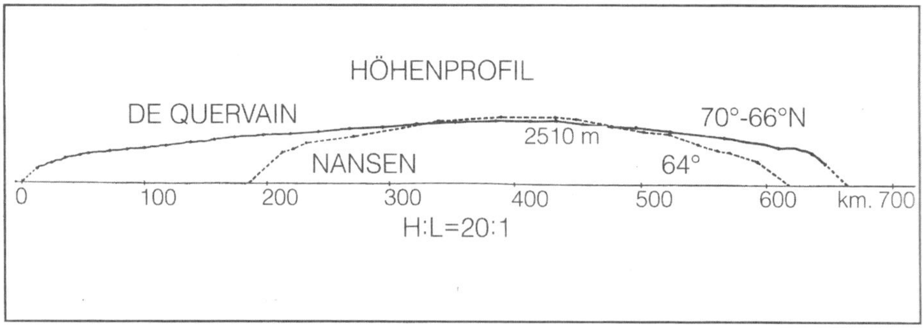

Figure 4
Altitude profile of the 1912 expedition's ice cap crossing.
Source: de Quervain, *Quer durchs Grönlandeis: Die Expeditionen 1909 und 1912/13*.

sheet margin and outlet glaciers. Two members of this western party, Wilhelm Jost and August Stolberg, wintered over in Greenland to make observations with weather balloons, thus contributing to an international research program coordinated with these activities. The strong scientific focus of the de Quervain expeditioners also manifests itself in their voluminous, detailed, and systematic research reports.

If the focus of the Swiss 1912 expedition was primarily scientific, we need to ask what it did for the scientific knowledge of its day and, further, if it had any lasting influence on the course of later research. Let us try to answer this question by giving a few examples related to our own field of glacier and ice sheet dynamics.

One of de Quervain's most important contributions was to make the first accurate cross-section of the Greenland ice sheet's shape and height. This profile was based on the detailed geodetic survey undertaken during the ice sheet crossing (FIGURE 4). Subsequently, these measurements have helped researchers develop basic concepts for the ice sheet's flow behaviour.

The expedition also made systematic and meticulous temperature and snow profile measurements during the crossing. These gave new insights into the spatial distribution of temperatures and snow accumulation across the ice sheet, showing that the inner ice sheet is a cold desert that accumulates only a few tens of centimetres of snow each year.

Almost a century later, these data have also served as essential constraints for maps of snow accumulation on the Greenland ice sheet.[2] And researchers continue to use them to calibrate models for estimating the mass balance of the ice sheet's surface – in other words, how far melting exceeds snow accumulation or vice versa.

Using the expedition's measurements, de Quervain was also able, for the first time, to determine the mass budget across the ice sheet, demonstrating that this vast polar ice cap was then roughly in balance. Besides providing important insights into how polar ice sheets work, these early measurements serve as a historical reference for assessing today's rapid retreat and mass loss of the Greenland ice sheet.

From the early 2000s, satellite and other observations revealed that the Greenland ice sheet's outlet glaciers were rapidly retreating and thinning. At the same time, the ice sheet's surface has been melting at an accelerating pace, so that Greenland is currently shedding its ice at a rate equivalent to losing more than twice the mass of all the glaciers in the European Alps every year. This melt raises sea levels around the world by about one millimetre annually.

At just a couple of decades, this period of observed rapid mass loss is difficult to interpret in terms of the centuries-long time scales that usually characterize climate projections. Early surveys are thus particularly valuable as a reference point for today's rapidly changing ice sheet. The measurements made by de Quervain's expedition more than a century ago are a case in point. Importantly, his observations support the view that the Greenland ice sheet was roughly in balance for a century or more before the onset of today's rapid mass loss.

The Swiss 1912 expedition made additional contributions. Its western party spent the summer investigating the Eqip Sermia, a glacier that flows into the sea at the western edge of the ice sheet. Their experiences are described in the chapter by their leader, Paul-Louis Mercanton, at the end of this book.

The western party's detailed survey allowed later researchers to show that the position of the glacier's terminus and its flow speed did not change much for many decades after the 1912 measurements.[3] This implies that the rapid retreat seen in the last decade, and the threefold increase in the glacier's flow rate, are phenomena that had never occurred during the previous century.

When we made our own field expedition to West Greenland in 2018, the western party's maps and meticulously documented observations[4] actually allowed us to repeat the surveys of the ice sheet margin profiles from exactly the same positions. We could even use the original reference points of the 1912 season in our surveys, as these points are still easily visible as cairns in the landscape.

The 1912 expedition is important not only for the data collected but also for the way that the researchers went about collecting them. Mercanton's western party, for example, applied state-of-the-art survey techniques originally developed for charting Swiss glaciers. They also used the new technique of stereo-photogrammetry to make accurate topographic maps of the ice sheet margin and small glaciers. The precision of these surveys makes them invaluable for assessing changes in today's ice sheet and glaciers, giving us the start of a unique century-long time series for ice fluctuations in Greenland.

De Quervain himself was an innovator in meteorological observation methods. Back in 1905, he had devised the first theodolite specifically designed to track weather balloons. This device became the standard method for determining air flows in the upper atmosphere. The western party's observations, made in synchrony with balloon launches in Iceland, filled a large gap in the experimental data, allowing the researchers to overturn the then widely accepted theory of a stagnant high-pressure system over the Greenland ice sheet.

De Quervain's 1912 expedition also bequeathed a practical legacy to future scientific parties. His relatively safe and convenient access point to the ice sheet via the Eqip Sermia glacier was exploited by many of his successors. These included Alfred Wegener in his 1929 and 1930 expeditions, and the French expeditions from 1948 to 1953. These ventures led to the European international glaciological expeditions (known as EGIG) from 1957 to 1960, in which de Quervain's son, Marcel, took part and which paved the way for today's collaborative European ice core research program.

While they took the same or similar routes to the ice cap, the later expeditions differed radically from de Quervain's model in their logistics and use of mechanized transport. Wegener experimented, unhappily, with propeller-driven sledges on his last two expeditions, while the French expeditions travelled across the ice cap in the tracked vehicles known as Weasels, using aircraft for surveys and resupply. By contrast, the Swiss 1912 expedition was minimalistic in both style and execution. De Quervain placed his trust in a small team with solid mountaineering and survival skills.[5] And, unlike almost all his successors, he depended heavily on the expertise, equipment, and even clothing of the native Greenlanders. From them, the expeditioners learned how to drive the dog sledges and handle the kayaks on which their lives depended.

De Quervain also employed local people as scouts, porters, and messengers. A close engagement with the Greenlanders and their knowhow, though much less so for his successors, was a matter of necessity for him. This relationship also helps to account for the respect and understanding he shows in his book when portraying the communities visited by the expeditioners on their way to and from the ice cap.

The 1912 expedition soon led to new lines of research in the Swiss Alps. In 1914, de Quervain started the systematic monitoring of snow accumulation and ice ablation on the Claridenfirn, which continues to this day,[6] yielding valuable insights into the long-term effects of climate change on glaciers. And, as we have seen, his interest in the climatology of the upper atmosphere led ultimately to the establishment of the Jungfraujoch high-alpine observatory.

Above all, de Quervain's expedition laid the foundations for Switzerland's tradition of polar science. His example inspired many young scientists of later generations, such as Fritz Müller, who led a series of expeditions to Axel Heiberg Island in the Canadian Arctic from 1959, or Atsumu Ohmura, whose expedition from the Swiss Federal Institute of Technology in Zurich investigated the equilibrium line of the Greenland ice sheet during the 1990s. Ohmura's expedition inaugurated the current Swiss Camp meteorological observatory, which is located not far from the track of de Quervain's ice cap crossing.

Appropriately, the 1912 expedition's legacy is commemorated by the annual Prix de Quervain, awarded to young polar scientists in Switzerland by the Swiss Committee on Polar and High Altitude Research, a body of the Swiss Academies of Arts and Sciences.

The continued involvement of Swiss scientists in polar research led to the establishment of the Swiss Polar Institute in 2016, a move that helped in the following year to prepare the way for Switzerland's accession to observer status in the Arctic Council, an intergovernmental forum for the circumpolar states. Fittingly, this book has been published with the institute's encouragement and support.

We would like to close on a personal note. Whenever we step onto the ice sheet during our own field work in West Greenland, we think back with gratitude and respect to de Quervain and his fellow pioneers of the Swiss 1912 expedition. And we will never cease to be amazed by how much science they achieved with such slender means.

NOTES

1 Pfäffli, "Das Wissen, das aus der Kälte kam," 30.

2 Atsumu Ohmura and Niels Reeh, "New Precipitation and Accumulation Maps for Greenland," *Journal of Glaciology* 37, no 125 (1991).

3 M. P. Luethi, A. Vieli, L. Moreau, I. Joughin, M. Reisser, D. Small, and M. Stober, "A Century of Geometry and Velocity Evolution at Eqip Sermia, West Greenland," *Journal of Glaciology* 62, no. 234 (2016): 640–54.

4 A. de Quervain and P-L. Mercanton, *Résultats scientifiques de l'expédition suisse au Groenland 1912–1913* (Copenhagen: Bianco Lunos Bogtrykkeri, offprint from *Meddelelser om Grønland* [Monographs on Greenland], no. 59, 1925).

5 Pfäffli, "Das Wissen, das aus der Kälte kam," 102.

6 M. Huss, A. Bauder, A, Linsbauer, J. Gabbi, G. Kappenberger, U. Steinegger, and D. Farinotti, "More Than a Century of Direct Glacier Mass-Balance Observations on Claridenfirn, Switzerland," *Journal of Glaciology* 3, no. 11 (2021): 1–17.

ABOUT THE COLOUR PLATES

The Swiss 1912 expeditioners rank among the pioneers of colour photography in the polar regions. As soon as they landed in Godthaab on Greenland's west coast, they set to work to develop some colour pictures in a local photographer's laboratory.

This was just half a year after Herbert Ponting had experimented with the same type of plate in the Antarctic, using a colour process launched on the market by the Lumière brothers of Lyon in 1907.[1] Alas, Captain Scott was unimpressed with the results, and no so-called Autochromes appeared in the published account of his last expedition.

Alfred de Quervain seems to have shared these misgivings. Only one Autochrome appeared in the first edition of *Quer durchs Grōnlandeis*, his book about the 1912 expedition. For Captain Scott was right: with their long exposure periods and often underwhelming tints, Autochromes were unready for prime time.

Yet colour images would be invaluable for reaching a wider public – particularly for the slide lectures that de Quervain and his expedition doctor, Hans Hössli, would give all over Switzerland in an effort to pay off some of the expedition's debts.

De Quervain squared this circle by taking the expedition's black-and-white glass plates to Wilhelm Heller, a professional retoucher working at Sumatrastrasse 3, Zurich.[2] Heller then hand-tinted them. All of the pictures reproduced for this English version of de Quervain's book were hand-tinted from these black-and-white glass slides – some of which have suffered from the passage of time (see plate 2, for example).

Scott's nemesis, Roald Amundsen, also resorted to hand-colouring his black-and-white photographs. But de Quervain probably followed the example of Arnold Heim. This Zurich-based geologist had travelled with de Quervain's group during their 1909 reconnaissance expedition, accompanying them for part of their sea journey northwards along the Greenland coast. In fact, several of Heim's colour images are featured in this book. They include, for example, the engaging picture of Inuit children at Nugsuak, reproduced here as plate 9. The same picture adorns the cover of Heim's account of his summer travels in Greenland, co-authored with the botanist Martin Rikli and published in 1911 as *Sommerfahrten in Grönland*.

Having never visited Greenland, the photographic retoucher who worked for de Quervain had to rely on his patron's guidance to arrive at an appropriate palette. In this sense, the colours you see in these plates represent the very hues of memory itself.

NOTES

1 Elizabeth Watkins, "Mapping the Antarctic: Photography, Colour and the Scientific Expedition in Exhibition," in *Progress in Colour Studies: Cognition, Language and Beyond*, edited by Lindsay MacDonald, Carole Biggam, and Galina V. Paramei (Amsterdam: John Benjamins, 2018).

2 See introduction by Peter Haffner in Alfred de Quervain, *Quer durchs Grönlandeis: Die Expeditionen 1909 und 1912/13* (1914; reprint, Zürich: Verlag Neue Zürcher Zeitung, 1998).

A NOTE ON THE TEXT

The translation published here was completed in 1983 by Alfred de Quervain's daughter Elisabeth de Quervain Schriever, with help from her husband, William. Both were Canadian citizens with Swiss roots. When editing their original typescript, we sought as far as possible to preserve the character of their text, in the hope that something of the author's voice and style will ring through from the underlying German.

In doing so, we have chosen to retain the word "Eskimo" where it was used by the author and his translators. It is clear from his usage of the word, which he frequently interchanges with the term "Greenlanders," that Alfred de Quervain meant no disrespect for the island's Indigenous peoples. On the contrary, his regard and affection for the Greenlandic way of life shines through his two expedition books.

Indeed, as Andreas Vieli and Martin Lüthi point out above, de Quervain and his companions owed their lives and success to their adoption of Inuit knowhow and to the wholehearted support of local communities – whose way of life the Swiss explorers strove to document before it vanished forever. We hope that readers will accept their account in the same enquiring and generous spirit in which it was originally presented.

ACROSS GREENLAND'S ICE CAP

ALFRED DE QUERVAIN

with contributions by

PAUL-LOUIS MERCANTON

and **AUGUST STOLBERG**

TRANSLATORS' FOREWORD

This book was translated by E.Q. Schriever and W.R. Schriever for Beatrice, Alfred, and Silvia Schriever. It will give you a glimpse of a moment in the life of your grandfather. Alfred de Quervain was born in 1879 near Berne and died in 1927 in Zurich in the midst of a full and active life. He was a physicist, by profession a meteorologist and a glaciologist and, as were many of his generation, a man of wide interests and broad knowledge.

Elisabeth de Q. Schriever
Ottawa, December 1983

AUTHOR'S PREFACE

Many of the friends of our expedition at home and abroad expressed the wish for an account of our experiences. And so we wrote this book in order to express our thanks to them.

Furthermore, our book is dedicated to all those who are interested in the Far North, not only because of the ice and snow but because of the purely human values that manifest themselves in so many ways in close contact with the forces of nature and the struggle against them.

It would be of special significance on our voyage that our route would take us not just from rock to ice and from ice to rock, like those of many other expeditions in Antarctica and the Arctic. We took our leave from a "people of nature" in the west, crossed the ice cap, and ended our journey in contact with an even more genuinely untouched people. It was astonishing to experience how civilized urban folk had to surrender to the forces of nature up there, how we began to love these natural people and to adapt and simplify our own way of life.

Although it was privately financed, we called our expedition "Swiss." This expressed one of my main ideas when I made my plans: the thought that we were particularly qualified to work in the polar region by our heritage, our love for the high mountains, and our familiarity with snow and glaciers, together with a certain adaptability and a bent for simplicity.

Our expectations were not disappointed. It may be deceptive that our success seemed to come relatively easily, almost as a matter of course. Our only aim was to carry out our program. On the one hand, we took great risks. But, on the other, we were so exact in devising and working out our preparations that perhaps some interesting but avoidable situations did not occur. For such would have been sensational and not to the credit of a serious undertaking.

We can be satisfied with our scientific results, of which we give a short outline at the end of the book.

A. de Quervain
Zürich, 7 October 1913

CHAPTER 1
PLANS AND PREPARATIONS

Greenland evokes nostalgia, not only in those who have lived there but also in European travellers such as ourselves. When we leave the country, we can hardly imagine never seeing any of it ever again.

Somehow, after my first voyage in 1909 with Dr A. Stolberg and Dr E. Baebler, an idea stuck in my mind. We had worked extremely hard, and we had essentially achieved what we had planned. But our foray onto the ice cap in the difficult Karajak region had taken us to the threshold of greater challenges, showing us how much more work there was to do, and how we could go about it, and also that we were able and qualified to do so.

We were prepared, and we had the experience to embark on a further exploration of the Greenland inland ice cap. Why should this experience now lie fallow at a moment when interest in Greenland had moved into the foreground of Arctic research?

Greenland's scale, as the largest island on earth, is not its most important geographic feature. It is not only for its area of two million square kilometres that it deserves to be called a continent. The country's most interesting feature is, as we shall see, its topography, which is unique in the northern hemisphere. Only Antarctica presents an analogous type of terrain, although yet vaster and mightier.

The Antarctic explorations of recent years and decades have revealed a continental highland almost entirely covered by a permanent ice cap at the South Pole. It seems that some of these expeditions were motivated primarily by the ambition of reaching the South Pole. (Let me remark here that it would be nonsense to speak of "discovering" the pole; no point can be discovered whose existence and position is already well defined.)

These trips have shown us how very different our two polar regions are. The North Pole is, against all expectations, a broad deep-sea basin. The South Pole, again unexpectedly, is a massive, high, connected landmass, covered by an ice cap. These contrasts produce substantial variations from the anticipated polar climatic pattern.

Yet the differences between the northern and southern polar areas are not quite absolute, if one does not limit the comparison to the immediate polar region but extends one's radius somewhat. Among the mostly low-lying landmasses that surround the Arctic Ocean, there is one vast mountainous area that extends 2,200 kilometres from north to south and is buried under an enormous glacier. It is nearly as high as Antarctica and influences the polar climate and the whole atmospheric circulation in a similar fashion. This is Greenland, the Arctic continent *par excellence*. It is in a way an "Antarctica" shifted from a polar to a sub-polar position, with a different set of problems posed by the inland ice cap.

The special position that Greenland holds within the circumpolar countries has always intrigued scientists, who feel especially attracted by the mystery of the inland ice cap.

Serious attempts to advance onto the ice cap are relatively recent. The first were by Lars Dalager in 1851 and Jens Arnold Jensen in 1878, in South Greenland. At a time when ice-climbing skills were not very advanced, Jensen's party managed to reach some isolated *nunataks*.[1] Later, Baron von Nordenskjöld's advance in 1883 was stopped after about one hundred kilometres by large "ice marshes." He could only send two Laplanders ahead, who came back with tales of enormous distances achieved but without having found the oases that Nordenskjöld had hoped to find.

Three years later, Robert Peary tried to penetrate Greenland from Disko Bay, and in 1888 Fridtjof Nansen and five companions did cross South Greenland. Five years afterwards, Harald Moltke, Vilhelm Garde, and Johan Petersen examined the south tip of the ice cap.

Peary made a series of trips by sled, mainly in 1892–95, and then explored the northern limit of the ice cap and the north end of the island of Greenland

1 Summits or high ridges of a mountain protruding from an ice field or glacier. Footnotes subscribed EQS, for Elisabeth de Quervain Schriever, are by the book's translators; other footnotes subscribed AdQ are by the author. The remainder are by the editors of this edition.

itself. His results will have to be modified somewhat in view of the latest long sledge trips that Knud Rasmussen made in this area in 1912.

The information that reached us about the southern region, indicating that the ice cap holds many surprises, stimulated us more than anything to undertake a new crossing of the Greenland ice cap to the north of Nansen's route. This traverse had so far been the basis of our knowledge of the ice cap, yet it did not seem acceptable to judge the island, which stretches another fifteen hundred kilometres to the north, only by this one cross-section.

Considering our preliminary work and our experience, we felt we could make a contribution to this country's exploration.

In my plans, I instinctively followed the exploration program that Peary had drawn up twenty-five years ago, which foresaw two more crossings, one in the middle and one in northern Greenland. The latter was already planned by the Danish expedition of Captain Johan Koch. This coincidence proved to be very advantageous for a division of work. To cross central Greenland had become much more feasible since Denmark had opened the trading post of Angmagssalik near the Arctic Circle, in order to keep alive the only remaining Eskimo settlement in East Greenland. Just once a year, a small ship docks there at the end of August, when the belt of pack ice is most likely to allow its passage.

If this point on the east coast were taken as either the start or the end point of an expedition, there would be no need to equip a special ship. This was a deciding factor, as I knew from the outset that we would have only modest financial means at our disposal. Under different circumstances, we would have preferred the route to Scoresby Sound, which is the same distance.

The choice of direction was also of great importance – that is, from the west coast to the east coast or vice versa.

Looking from Europe, it seems closer and safer to start at the only inhabited place on the east coast, Angmagssalik, and to aim at the more populous west coast. But as the ship reaches Angmagssalik at the end of August or in September, it would then be too late to start a crossing that same year. We would have to spend the winter on the east coast and add a whole year to our schedule.

If we crossed in the other direction, the expedition could set out from the west coast early in summer, carefully taking advantage of all conditions, in order to reach the east coast in time for the ship's arrival. However, we would have to reach the only inhabited point on the east coast or perish. In addition, there was the unfortunate fact that this inhabited point is situated on an island, roughly sixty kilometres from the location where it was easiest to reach the coast from the inland ice, separated by the broad and ice-choked Sermilik Fjord. A special depot of supplies would have to be pre-positioned on the coast.

Despite these considerable difficulties, I decided to take the latter route. When I was in Greenland in 1909, I had already worked out the plan and had given a written outline to the inspector of North Greenland. Whether I would be able to carry it out, considering my health and my obligation as a federal employee, was another question.

Quite unexpectedly, I was given a good round sum of money that obliged me to carry on. I found understanding and encouragement for my plan from the well-known glaciologist Professor F.A. Forel and the president of the Geneva Geographical Society, Professor R. Gautier. They encouraged me to seek support inside the country, and not abroad, where money would have been easier to find, in order to organize a *Swiss* expedition. Knowing this, I felt confident that I could keep the costs sufficiently low that funds could certainly be raised in Switzerland.

I soon found out it was not that easy. Even foundations for scientific travel were unable to help. One well-endowed foundation at the Federal Institute of Technology paid only for the travels of full professors with tenure, not of lecturers, while the travel grants of the federal government were solely for biological research. It is not the custom, nor would it be proper for me, a mere youngster, to levy criticisms of our higher institutions, but it is interesting to mention these oddities to illustrate certain difficulties in our preparations.

At the time, I was still hoping for some federal subsidies, since the expedition had been recommended to the Federal Council by the Schweizerische Naturforschende Gesellschaft (SNG). In the meantime, the SNG went ahead and collected a sizable sum at its yearly meeting, where Professor F.A. Forel, young at heart, very touchingly went around and canvassed himself. Three days later, in August, I had to be in Copenhagen and used the whole sum on the supplies for the depot to be set up on the east coast. By an extraordinarily fortunate coincidence, I met Administrator Petersen of Angmagssalik, who was on home leave in Copenhagen for the first time in many years before returning to his solitude for an indefinite period. I was able to make important arrangements with him. We decided to set up a cache on the Sermilik Fjord at a specific point that we could identify opposite Umitujarajuit, a small island and the only one marked on the map. It was obvious that Petersen was a man on whom we could rely. So much depended on this. What particularly charmed me was his laconic parting remark, without sentiment or rhetoric: "See you next year!"

By the time winter arrived, all that the expedition could call its own were my leave from work, the valuable permission of the Danish government to travel in Greenland, obtained with the help of the Swiss Federal Council, and a depot of supplies on the east coast. But what good would a depot in the east be when the means to reach even the west coast didn't yet exist? Only the polar bears would stand to benefit.

The hot summer of 1911, as happy as it may have been in my personal life,[2] seemed to extinguish more and more of our financial hopes. At the critical moment, drought and emergency conditions very severely crimped the customs revenues of the federal government, quashing any hopes of a federal grant.[3] Leave of absence by itself was not helpful. At this difficult juncture, the Geneva Geographical Society and the SNG Zurich agreed to do further fundraising, which in turn prompted the *Neue Zürcher Zeitung* newspaper to guarantee 10,000 Swiss francs. This was enough to start the expedition on its way.

Other scientific groups, private citizens, and the expedition members themselves dug into their pockets to help reach the goal of 30,000 Swiss francs, the total amount needed. Despite all the careful management, the final costs would be one-third higher, mainly because we extended our program. We later tried to cover the deficit by giving lectures, and the Kaiser Wilhelm University in Strasburg[4] gave its former lecturer a generous contribution.

Regarding the project's chances of success, opinions differed. My friends in Zurich wanted to know what should be done if we did not come out on the east coast. My answer was that nothing could or should be done. From Greenland came a letter from a prominent personality to whom I had sent my travel plan. He called this undertaking presumptuous and maintained that its implementation would lead to certain death. This pronouncement reached me very appropriately on the day of my engagement, a good reason to put it silently *ad acta*.

On the other hand, there were the more positive remarks of other explorers such as Otto Nordenskjöld and Erich von Drygalski, who fully concurred with our plans and thus encouraged us.

Organizing an expedition is like setting up a building on suspect terrain. Half the planning and attention must be concentrated on the foundation, preparations that later are hardly noticed unless they prove inadequate. I can say that there was not one piece of equipment that wasn't carefully considered, researched, and tested.

First, we had to acquire measuring instruments, both for the group traversing the ice cap and for those who would remain on the west coast to make the

---

2 He got married (EQS).

3 Customs duties are the main income of the federal government, income tax being a cantonal prerogative (EQS).

4 Alsace was then a German province (EQS).

glaciological measurements and for the two men who planned to spend the winter doing atmospheric observations. We were able to borrow a number of instruments from helpful scientific institutes and private persons, but we needed good chronometers. This worry was taken off our minds when the top chronometer manufacturers, Paul Ditisheim and Ulysse Nardin, put their best products at our disposal, without consideration of the enormous risk. When these shiny little things, ticking innocently and dreamily in their beds of mahogany and satin, first were first presented to me, I almost felt sorry for them, thinking of the doubtful situations and unwholesome surroundings in which they would have to prove their excellence. But they did indeed prove that they came from good houses. Whether they stood on their heads or swam in icy water, they kept their time.

I won't mention all our instruments with the personal affection they deserve. That would be foolish. And yet, later, under certain circumstances we would value the real support and comfort we received from a reliable instrument. This is one place where one does not have to worry about dishonesty and disappointment. Instruments belong to a realm where a kind of universal world order exists. As I heard one physicist wistfully remark, "It is better to work with instruments than with people." Even if we do not give in to this kind of pessimism, it is clear that, gambling our lives on the reliability of instruments as we did, we would develop a special, almost human, relationship with them.

Next in importance after the instruments came the technical equipment. Here we benefited from the experience of our previous expedition. I had four slightly improved Nansen sleds made, four metres long, with precisely fitted instrument cases and equipment bags. The suggestions of my prospective companions were also very helpful. Together we devised a practical tent that would later serve as a model for the Zurich botanical study group to the Caucasus. The manufacturer told me at the time that he was making one hundred thousand tents for the Bulgarian and Serbian armies. Several days later, while examining distance-measuring meters for our expedition, I heard the same thing: "All for the Bulgarian army." I cannot really claim now that I then thought this to be somewhat remarkable.[5]

I was quite aware that, without anticipating the experience of the Turkish army, badly nourished troops would not be able to withstand the rigours of the ice cap. Relying on earlier experiences, I brought almost all our canned goods from Switzerland, and this worked extremely well. One important product,

5 Prior to World War I (EQS).

pemmican, I could only get in Copenhagen. Pemmican played such a key role in our existence – as it did in so many other expeditions – that I have to give it a special introduction. It solves the requirement for a food that is practical, relatively lightweight and nourishing in cold climates. Whether the taste buds are fulfilled is a question very much open to debate. The physiologist of the German polar expedition in the south found the taste to be a combination of sawdust and Vaseline. Visitors to the Greenland exhibition in Zurich always had the same horrified reaction, "Oh no! It tastes like soap." To be honest, most members of the expedition were also critical at first, until they got to know the product's true worth. To be exact, pemmican consists of one half chemically dried and ground-up beef and one half fat. On Nordenskjöld's advice, we fed the pemmican intended for human consumption to the dogs as well. This meant a considerable saving in weight on the crossing and so further supplies for ourselves.

Part of an expedition's "equipment" is its participants. I had never actively sought people out, being of the opinion that I could not ask anyone to take part in an undertaking whose considerable risks I alone could properly judge. But a good number of capable candidates from Switzerland, Germany, Austria, Belgium, and Norway turned up. From these, I chose three for the crossing of the ice cap, to make four of us in all. This seemed to be a practical number. In the case of illness or an accident to one member of the group, it would be possible for the remaining three to carry him along, so that such a mishap would not necessarily mean a partial or absolute catastrophe. In an extreme case, three could carry on. A group of four provides the further option of splitting temporarily into two groups without leaving one man on his own, an option that proved invaluable later on. To increase the number beyond the necessary minimum would not have been a good idea. The probability of including one less capable member increases with greater numbers.

My companions for the traverse were Dr Hans Hössli, MD, from St Moritz, and architect Roderich Fick and engineer Karl Gaule from Zurich. Of course, it was important for us to get to know each other beforehand. As the participants in such an undertaking should not meet on the boat for the first time, we did a trial camping trip to the Engadine in the middle of the winter, complete with Nansen sleds, tent, and sleeping bags. The three had all prepared themselves for their specific tasks, which led to an efficient division of scientific duties. Beside their scientific, professional knowledge, Fick and Gaule possessed all sorts of practical skills useful on an expedition, which they put to good use in our preparations. In Hössli I appreciated above all, besides his skills as an alpinist, his medical and surgical knowledge, which turned out to be very helpful.

To ensure our success, I felt that we four should not have to rely solely on ourselves on the difficult west coast of Greenland. The result was that a western party would be organized to accompany us a short distance onto the ice. They would then examine the rim zone of the ice cap near our departure point and take systematic glaciological measurements. It was obvious that the main team could not afford time for this research, although it would be an essential addition to its work.

Besides my old Greenland companion Dr August Stolberg, I was also able to enlist Professor Paul-Louis Mercanton from Lausanne who, as secretary of the International Glaciological Commission, would certainly be the best man to lead these investigations.

His assistant, Dr Wilhelm Jost from Bern, a very knowledgeable glaciologist and physicist, would do an excellent job, together with Dr Stolberg. These latter two were to remain in Greenland all winter in order to continue the atmospheric research that we had begun on the earlier expedition. They would be dealing in particular with research on the high-altitude airstreams of the polar region in winter, which are still largely uninvestigated.

I do not have to praise my companions. Our success speaks for itself. Such an achievement is possible only with a group of able people in whom quality of character is as important as physical fitness and scientific ability. Now that we have introduced all of us by name, the course of the story will no doubt reveal more details of our personalities.

Besides the active members of the expedition, I want to remember the associate members, all of whom I cannot name here. I thank them all – who shared their knowledge, gave their time, their instruments, skis, dried apples, bacon, socks, and honey. And I must not forget a little box of brandy, given by a dear but old-fashioned friend. He probably vaguely remembered from books he read in his youth that there were mysterious connections between this elixir and northern excursions. But it so happened – maybe not quite by coincidence – that, among the seven of us, four and a half were teetotallers. Fick didn't even know the taste of wine. While the others did not turn down a taste when in central Europe, they could easily forgo it on the expedition without complaints. So the noble brandy box made the return trip untouched, while the excellent non-alcoholic wines from Meilen and Briod, which embellished our little parties, did not by any means remain untouched.

Let us now move ahead to the time when all these things and a lot more are packed in about a hundred boxes and crates and stowed deep in the innards of the *Hans Egede*, which is ready to depart. Let us skip over the time of packing, telegraphing, and worrying over baggage pieces that were mislaid or held up because of the coal strike of the day. And let us go on board ourselves.

I would like to recall a talk I had shortly before leaving with Commander Gustav Holm, who had led the so-called women's boat expedition to the east coast thirty years earlier and had mapped the part of the coast where we planned to come out. I found out that unfortunately he had not been able to visit the exact region where we planned to descend from the ice cap. He had only seen it from a distance and had drawn the details on the map based on what the Eskimos had described.[6] It is from the details on this map that we had chosen the place for the depot, and with this map that we expected to find it. There was supposed to be a large island with the beautiful name Kekertatsuatsiak and to the left of it a smaller one called Umitujarajuit, a name that was by now quite familiar to us. Incidentally, I found out later that there were two or three more difficult syllables missing in this name. At that moment, though, it was not the etymological but rather the cartographical detail that worried me:

Did the large island exist at all?

"Maybe, but possibly not."

Was he sure the small island existed?

"Maybe."

The last thing the amiable commander called after me, as I was taking my leave: "Don't rely on the map on any account. Do not trust the map."

Well, this was going to be something! If the little island did not exist, where would Petersen, who also believed in the existence of Umitujarajuit, put the depot?

It was most important for me to learn from Commander Holm himself under what circumstances, and from where, the critical area had been surveyed. But his farewell words sounded ominous, and I decided to keep them to myself. Often they would ring in my ears, and later we were reminded of them with body and soul.

6 This is the word used in the original and the translation – also used in modern days by Barry Lopez in *Arctic Dreams*. It would be anachronistic to use "Inuit," which has the stamp of late twentieth-century usage.

CHAPTER 2
THE SEA VOYAGE

This year the departure of the Greenland steamer was postponed from the traditional first day of April to the second. They probably did not want to leave early on a Monday because farewell parties on Sunday night, celebrated with special intensity by many sailors considering their distant and frigid destination, might have a detrimental effect on their course and eagerness to travel the next day.

Old French mariners had a fervent prayer:

Seigneur ayez pitié des pauvres marins à terre,
Sur mer ils se débrouilleront bien tout seuls.[1]

As far as the passengers' eagerness to travel went, we all knew that, eager or not, the result would be the same in the end.

Early in the morning, indecently early for Copenhagen and in foul weather, the *Hans Egede* weighed anchor. Counting heads as usual, I found six instead of seven. Mercanton was missing, and the captain did not look as if he intended to wait for latecomers. Just before the gangway to the doubtful paradise of Greenland was withdrawn, there he was, silently deprecated yet fervently anticipated. He'd had some important and urgent business, he explained, and we believed every word. Of course. As a matter of fact, our dear Mercanton acquired the nickname Je-viens-tout-de-suite for the expedition's duration.

---

1 Lord have mercy on the poor sailors ashore, / At sea they will manage quite well on their own.

This little interlude had the advantage – or disadvantage – that only as we were slowly moving off did I have the time to reflect again how strange it was that I was going away into this grey future, leaving my wife standing in the blowing snow, alone on the pier. But soon we had waved enough. We had to think ahead and hold our first "war council" to assign jobs while we were still all functioning.

This didn't last long. Is it necessary to describe another Atlantic crossing? If you are calling to mind the colossus on which you are ferried to New York, as if on a floating island, without being able to distinguish the waves from the promenade deck, and without missing any amenity to which you are accustomed on dry land, then I would not bother to repeat it. Whoever travels that way scarcely acquaints themselves with wind and waves.[2]

But if you travel at the tail-end of winter into a North Atlantic storm, swaying in a nutshell of a boat like our Greenland steamer, you will have tales to tell of unforgettable experiences, although more of defeat than of victory.

The awkward truth is that memory gilds and falsifies recollections. I therefore decided to record, at all times and as well I could, what we felt at the moment. I share with you a few samples of what I wrote down *de profundis* "without regard to mental and physical anguish," as far as the original text, which sometimes disintegrates into illegible dots and lines, can be reconstructed.

8 APRIL 1912, *Hans Egede*

On the day of our departure, I started to write a few lines in my diary. I have no idea where they are. How could anyone know anything now? Above all, this is the seventh day of our voyage through this watery desert, of our vegetating on this restless, rocking tub. And today is worse than ever.

Time generally passes in a grey stupor. However, nobody has lost their sense of humour altogether, but it is a grim sort of humour. In the morning when we "wake up," we lie in our cabins with throbbing heads. One persuades oneself to take a little oatmeal – the only thing that stays down, as we found out by trial and error. The basic wish not to move at all is replaced by another even stronger wish as hours pass, to relieve the neck which hurts from endless tossing around and being tossed. Finally, one tries, without enthusiasm, and not without risk, to climb down from the bunk and to move oneself to the deck, past dangerous smells emanating from the open provisions room.

Only the uppermost part of the deck near the funnel is safe. Everything else is swamped again and again, often a foot deep.

---

2 A week later, the *Titanic* went down (EQS).

There one sits for an hour or two, clinging with both hands to the grate over the hatch, resignedly watching the enormous waves as they roll past. Or one walks with hasty, uncertain steps up and down the narrow space, never sure when one will suddenly have to spend more time than one wishes bent over the railing.

"Oh, que trois fois et quatre fois heureux sont ceux qui plantent des choux! Car ils ont toujours un pied sur terre ferme, et l'autre n'est pas loin!"[3] Mercanton never tires of quoting from Gargantua's ocean voyage by Rabelais. Oh, how he speaks for all of us – at least the ones who understand French.

One thing is sure. The destiny of the expedition does not lie on the water. Except for Mercanton. He is indestructible and never misses a meal, while we at best manage an unambiguous gesture of refusal when the dinner bell rings and Arthur, the young cabin boy, comes and asks: *Vil de komme at spise?*

Mercanton in his unshakable good health and – this does not automatically follow – his kind and obliging way is a gift to the expedition. But when he sits on deck with all the disappointed souls, talking, singing, reciting, and playing his flute, some of us in our reduced frame of mind may feel a little overwhelmed, especially if we do not quite understand this *exubérance romande*. Yesterday Gaule fled to another bench, totally worn out.

Mercanton, together with Jost, who is relatively vigorous as well, makes daily meteorological observations. He also tries to receive wireless signals from Paris at midnight.

Among us, Hössli is the least hale or hearty. Today he talked about the day of his birth in connection with ocean voyages and seasickness in a downright negative way.

Stolberg, widely travelled, lives through it all with great composure. Fick and Gaule suffer through the general misery without loud complaints, though not with Stolberg's experience and equanimity.

They say there were northern lights in the night from Saturday to Sunday. We looked for some reflection of them today, Easter Monday. We distributed my brother Theodor's apples and Mrs Mercanton's coloured Easter eggs. Yesterday, Mercanton brought me a book on Neobuddhism, which deals with the existence of great general suffering and tries to find the root of it. Anyone who travelled for eight days on the *Hans Egede* can answer this question in a flash and will formulate it as Stolberg's axiom: "There is too much water!"

My clothes must contain enough salt to supply a whole household. First there are the breakers on deck. Then there was the deluge through the porthole, opened

3 Oh, thrice and four times happy are those who plant cabbages! / For they always have one foot on firm ground, and the other is not far away!

secretly and foolishly, which led to a triple hermetic sealing of the porthole for the rest of the trip after we had to confess to the *jomfru* (maid).

"Oh que trois fois, et quatre fois heureux sont ceux qui plantent des choux …"

TUESDAY, 9 APRIL

After I managed to compose the above prose yesterday, I worked my way up on deck and found the waves still high. But this time the sun shone brightly. There was a strong north wind, and we were on the backward side of a low pressure system, the centre of which had passed to the south during the night. Everybody started to recover. Unfortunately, feathery clouds soon appeared in the western sky again, harbingers of a new storm. And in these latitudes at sea, it does not take long. By evening, the wind had shifted to the west and the sky was overcast. It is amazing how accurately even small barometric changes are accompanied by corresponding changes in cloud formations and wind directions.

Today is totally grey once more, without much wind, although the sea is in perpetual motion and the *Hans Egede* is restless. Gaule trusted the lull too far and started taking measurements of atmospheric electricity, at least until the *Hans Egede* threw over his apparatus.

Gaule's dynamometer, a small instrument that measures the power of one's grip, plays quite a large role in our daily existence. The strength of your hand changes, of course, with your state of health. Jost gets the best results, up to sixty-eight kilograms, but Fick and Gaule are not far behind, while the average for the ship's crew is around forty-two. It is with pride that I see what mighty men have rallied around the flag of the expedition … now I am out of ink!

WEDNESDAY, 10 APRIL

I found no fresh ink yesterday but ate my first meal with confidence. There was a mouth-organ concert by Mercanton and Hössli. We have little wind and the waves are small, but a great swell comes from the northeast. While the ship's propeller churns out its half-second beat, my small porthole goes up and down, always four seconds high above the waterline showing the distant grey horizon, then four seconds down until the green waters cover it and swish by. And so on, ad infinitum: one two three four, one two three four …

This morning Stolberg and I, whose bunks are at the same level, felt well enough to start a discussion on the possible existence of an Alsatian culture in general and the conditions for a dual culture in particular.[4]

4 Stolberg lived in Alsace, and de Quervain had taught there for a few years (EQS).

Hössli, with his German-Romansch-Italian background, added his opinions from the lower bunk. We asked if we were a nation. So many nuances of the discussion are irrevocably lost, since I could only take short notes. I was still hovering in a half-stupor where thoughts started to take form but could not be readily grasped and expressed.

Afternoon. We huddle in the so-called smoking salon, an extension of the "breathing hole," as the hatch over the gangway is called. This is Jost's and Hössli's home, while the tribe from the Zürichberg has settled on the iron grill behind the smokestack, more for warmth from the boiler room than for the accompanying smell of burned oil. I would call them the thermotropic people in contrast to the more aerotropic ones.

We make good headway. In three days, we'll round Cape Farvel.[5]

At the table, the conversation among the Danes revolves exclusively around the metric system, which came into use on 1 April in Denmark. To us it seems almost comical to hear how the basic facts of litre and decilitre are very earnestly debated from all angles. We feel transported back to a far-off primary school time.

FRIDAY, 12 APRIL

Early. In my bunk. Another *Hans Egede* night. Nobody slept, but we suffered silently, until at 6 a.m. someone in the lower bunks vented his feelings explosively. "Sauschiff!" A strong expression, but I silently agree.

SATURDAY, 13 APRIL

Today we passed Cape Farvel. It wasn't visible, although I had waved it a hopeful "auf Wiedersehn" three years ago. In a stormy southwester, we turn into the Davis Strait. Yesterday I could stand it on deck till noon, but the mere sight of *fiskeboller*, a fish-pudding, the worst invention of Danish imagination, upset my equilibrium. Here I lie in my bunk with a throbbing head, barely able to think. Any remaining thoughts left travel in the past or far ahead of the ship into the unknown future and then back home again. It is the unknown that I dissect over and over again to find any possible weak spot in my plans that could be improved. The dogs? The east coast?

MONDAY, 15 APRIL

Hurrah! The coastal mountains of Greenland near Julianehaab and Ivigtut become visible, the Kungnait, Sernerut, and all the others, these marvellous

5 Cape Farewell on Canadian maps (EQS).

alpine peaks all snowed in. Now my men are convinced that we are in the right place, and they come alive. And so do I, for the first time. Yesterday Mercanton and I made the astronomical measurements to determine the ship's position and found it agreed exactly with the official one made with the ship's instruments. Mercanton, to whom these measurements were novel, was very pleased indeed. Now it is snowing again.

16 APRIL, evening, in the port of Godthaab

Before turning in, just two lines: Today was a splendid day. The weather was so beautiful that the Hjortetakken was visible early in the morning far off on the northern horizon and, in full view of the magnificent mountain scenery, we sailed into the harbour at 3:30 p.m.

Between 6 p.m. and 8 p.m. we walked to the town of Godthaab, half an hour away. There the seminarians gave a performance in their gymnasium in the expedition's honour. Jost became quite enthusiastic and started to explain in German, "See, that's the way, swing the right leg to the left … !" In the meantime, gentle Mercanton sat at the harmonium-organ and played the newest hit waltz from Copenhagen. The next day, half the colony was whistling it, and in no time it propagated up the whole coast.

In a fiery red sunset, we walked back along the coast to the ship, with the mountains Saddlen and Hjortetakken ahead of us. Everyone was impressed, and to top it all, there was a wonderful display of northern lights, moving bands with yellow, green, and red borders. We all stood, speechless.

While I never wished that any of you were with us on the sea voyage, now I wish you could see all this.

Everybody is in high spirits, but tomorrow we start our work.

CHAPTER 3
OLD FRIENDS

The Greenlandic Eskimos still exist today because, to its credit, the Danish government has held a guardian's hand over them for two centuries, keeping out unwanted intruders. Greenland is a forbidden land where only Danish officials employed by the Greenland administration and scientific travellers are admitted. All commerce lies entirely in the hands of the government, which therefore accepts a certain responsibility for the welfare and the existence of the Greenlanders. Even though this monopoly was certainly not always disinterested, well-intentioned efforts and considerable sacrifices have been made over the years to preserve this hunting people.

When we visited the first Greenland colony, I was pleased to notice that my companions, newly arrived in Greenland, had the same immediate reactions as Stolberg and I had previously and now felt again. It is a pleasure to come here, to see the friendly, good-natured faces and the sound relationship between Danes and Greenlanders. I have my doubts that the first impression in an African colony would be as harmonious.

We are amazed to meet these hunters still using primitive old weapons, yet to see that close contact with outside culture has not had the usual deadly effects. The first impression upon landing is one of laughter, almost comedy. The colourful leggings of the women may contribute to this impression. But the stark rocky land has, at sea level, the same climate as the high mountain peaks in the Alps, and this reminds any who plan to live here that they are watching not a theatre piece but a brutal struggle for existence.

The first impression is also deceptive in other ways. At first one takes Greenlanders for harmless children of nature, but it turns out that they are very ordinary human beings who can be more than adept at negotiating to their own advantage, despite a general dislike of arithmetic. They are not as "genuine" as one thinks at first sight. Only the Eskimos at Cape York and the Eastern Eskimos in Angmagssalik may still make this claim. The Western Eskimos are a mixed race, calling themselves Greenlanders and not Eskimos. The conditions in this Danish colony tend increasingly to erode the viability of a pure hunting culture. Experience also shows that a mixed race seems more ready to adapt to new ways of making a living. On the other hand, I found the following apparently contradictory remark in the journal of a Danish explorer: "The further from the colony a Greenlander travels, the more efficient he becomes."

For the visitor, there is a unique attraction in staying among these people. This is an experience that is entirely missing in Antarctica or in any other polar region. Even for the scientist who studies inanimate nature, there is no doubt that the most fascinating object of all is man himself.

The day after our arrival, we had a great deal of work to do. First, there were some official visits, a must even in Greenland, especially in a "town" such as Godthaab, where there must be a good dozen adult Danish colonists. Stolberg and I found old acquaintances who were happy to see us again. It was the same with the Greenlanders. Our old maid, Sabine, was touched and proud that we recognized her in the crowd, and there was Fredrick Heilman, our former Greenlander guide. Another unexpected acquaintance turned up. One man of the Greenlander ship's guards asked me in broken Danish if I knew a certain Hutterite missionary from Germany. He believed that everybody speaking German on the other side of the great water must be on the most familiar terms with each other. But then it turned out that he was the husband of our Sophia from Nordlyt. He was most astonished that I knew so much about his wife, her death three years ago, about his children, and even about the interior of his Greenlandic hut.

On the other hand, it was my turn to be astonished when I was told that the settlement of Nordlyt was to be abandoned, although it had played a vital role in Greenland's history for the best part of two hundred years. Of all the Greenlander huts, only one was inhabited, by an old woman, and the great old building that had served as the church, workshop, and living quarters of the Hutterites was going to be torn down. Even though to the average Central European the abandonment of this colony is of little import, the clearing of Nordlyt is an event of some significance to the Greenlander.

Our work was by no means limited to exchanging reminiscences of Greenland. We had a chance to use the darkroom of the Greenlander Jon Möller to develop our colour photographs. Mercanton and I recalibrated the barometer of the local meteorological station with our hypsometer. However, the local observer, a Greenlander, couldn't quite make the connection between our steaming apparatus and his barometer.

It was 8 p.m. when we returned to the ship we had left at 7 a.m., and we were glad to get some food into our stomachs.

The following day we planned to climb the Hjortetakken in order to give our circulation some vigorous exercise. The captain had offered us the use of a motorboat to get there. Because of a misunderstanding, the boat's skipper thought that his destination was a spot much closer by and that he was not allowed beyond this point. Due to the discussion and the return trip to get new orders, we lost valuable time, while clouds started to gather around Hjortetakken. But then we were under way, eager to stay out in the fresh air.

Instead of going straight up the big gully as we had done three years ago, we turned around the "smaller" Hjortetakken. We tried the ascent from the south, which ended in a big traverse over the cornice on the summit ridge.

The modest cairn that Baebler and I had built was still covered with snow that even now was whirling around us in the wind. There was no particular attraction to staying on the summit. However, the Swiss singing trio, Jost, Hössli, and Mercanton, could not be talked out of crooning a few well-known Swiss songs, and I couldn't keep from humming along, hoping that the rocks weren't particular about my harmonizing.[1]

Back in Godthaab, the administrator helped me buy from the Greenlanders four down jackets of a type made only in South Greenland. These are very light and warm and would be handy on the ice cap. However, Denmark has a monopoly on the sale of down. Although the jackets had all seen service on the back of a Greenlander, the official had serious scruples. He finally reasoned that there would not be much left of the down after crossing the ice cap. Besides, it is an open secret that the Greenlanders do a little trading on the side with sailors and travellers despite the monopoly and without really damaging the crown of Denmark. Only the blue fox and the polar bear on the east coast are off-limits.

On 19 April, the *Hans Egede* left Godthaab and sailed to Sukkertoppen. As the ship was going to stay there for a few days, we decided to use our time to go on an extended excursion to the mountains on the Sermilik Fjord. *Sermilik* is

1 He could not carry a tune at all (EQS).

a common name for a fjord in Greenland; it means a fjord into which a glacier flows and which has icebergs.

We pitched our tents near the end of the fjord, and the motorboat of the colony left us, promising to pick us up two days later. Just in case, we kept the rowing boat that the *Hans Egede* had lent us after we promised solemnly to treat it with respect.

For the first time we found ourselves absolutely alone in the wilderness, relying on our own resources. Before anything else, we had to organize the sleeping arrangements. The silk tent was too small for seven, so Hössli and I slept outside in our sleeping bags. As my diary records, "How magnificent it is to see the fading evening sky and the blue and pink glaciers which descend to the seashore! One only has to peek through a small slit in the sleeping bag. As a Benediction, Jost is singing a melancholy Emmental evensong and then finishes with a yodel out into the glaciated world of Greenland."

Are we a nation, we Swiss? This was a frequent topic in academic discussions back home. The answer cannot be argued out but must be felt. Here on this trip I experienced it: yes, we are! We ourselves are the proof of the pudding. Among us, Switzerland's cultural and linguistic regions were represented by quite varied and distinct characters. As for me, although I had spent my best years abroad where I had found so many scientific and personal friends, I experienced that this is not fiction but fact: Swiss people find themselves connected to other Swiss by something beyond the differences between the rapid French of the Romands and the less flowing Schwyzerdütsch of the German speakers. This is something not to be found beyond our own small homeland, no matter what else we may find out there in the wide world. And this indefinable something should be cherished. It was well worth several nights of meditation in a sleeping bag to arrive at this conclusion.

Early the next morning, 21 April, we set out on skis to gain a view of the mountains from a peak farther east. First, we crossed the four-part terminal moraine of a glacier that had withdrawn to the back of the valley, as if it were unhappy in these harsh modern times.

The foehn blew down the slopes from the east, chasing the menacing fog bank from the mountain peaks but also softening the snow for us. After reaching the summit of our ski hill, which, to our disappointment, was no higher than a thousand metres, we measured a base length of a few hundred metres on the narrow ridge. We needed this to take our bearings and for photogrammetric measurements. Although we had to tread carefully on the ridge and watch out to our left and our right, Jost and Hössli representing our expedition's mountaineers, way over on the left, were openly sneering at a so-called summit where you could measure out a trigonometric base length. Nevertheless, the view from this maligned top was magnificent, taking in snowfields and rock cliffs all around and, far to the east, land where for the most part nobody had ever walked or probably even seen.

Our group of *montagnards* skied down in one straight line over the now hard-frozen snow slopes to the fjord far below, whose dark waters lapped at the tongue of the craggy glaciers. The right-hand crew, representing the flat-landers, more mindful of the delicate instruments and the integrity of their own persons, wisely put some zigzags into their descent.

In the evening, our more serious conversation turned around sleeping bags. We had two kinds: bags of reindeer hide for the ice cap, and double woollen ones with air pillows for the west coast – the same type that Stolberg and I had used and appreciated three years ago. But it so happens that the younger, more demanding generation is never satisfied with the household wares of their grandparents' era, as Mercanton's notes will confirm. I might add that at this point not all the sleeping bags were available to us yet. Some in the tent had to make do with blankets. They eagerly pulled heather boughs from under the snow and from dry spots and lugged great masses of them into the tent and slept for twelve hours. I marvelled at the justice of this. Later they would have no need of heather mattresses. By then, we of the eastern party would have already learned how to sleep comfortably as and where we lay.

We didn't miss much that day on the Sermilik Fjord. The night helped in its way to round out our equipage by laying down a blanket of snow on tent and sleeping bags, transforming the sleepers outside into little, ill-defined snow mounds. A dense fog blotted out the landscape. When it lifted a little, we went by boat to the edge of the two glaciers that calve into the fjord and climbed up to the larger one. These glaciers do not originate on the ice cap. We were not even sure that the view to the horizon from our ski hill extended as far as the ice cap. We had here only glaciers formed from local accumulations of ice. Consequently, their movement is slow, and they do not shed much ice into the fjord.

It was already dark and the fjord started to freeze over again. We were prepared to spend another night outside when the motorboat from Sukkertoppen arrived to take us on the lengthy voyage through snow and wind back to the colony.

We cannot leave Sukkertoppen with the *Hans Egede* without mentioning the kind hospitality we found at the house of Administrator Hastrup and his wife. They made us welcome at their well-appointed table and at the piano. Concerning music and song, there is no melody we were to hear more often in Greenland than "Integer vitae." Starting here, it followed us on our way, and in the end welcomed us back on the east coast.

CHAPTER 4
THE DOG SCHOOL

After sailing northward for a day, we reached Holstensborg, our first destination, where we planned to stay for a month. There we would gladly have done without the bare earth: we had hoped for more snow on the ground. Snow would be essential for practising our sledging skills, which would be so crucial to our traverse of the ice cap that it topped our program for Holstensborg. But now the round hills surrounding the colony looked suspiciously dark, and only the heights of the Praestefjeld and bold Kjärlinghetten were still covered with snow.

Our first concern, though, was to get all our expedition gear unloaded in the single day that the impatient *Hans Egede* allowed us and then to transport everything far inland to the doctor's empty house. This had been offered to us by the local Danish official.

For the first time since we left Copenhagen, we could excavate the "layers of deposit" that had built up in our cabins. The cramped bunk of one member of the expedition who shall remain nameless yielded the following, according to the order of the official listing: one small and one large blanket made from bird feathers, three earmuffs, one fur collar, three dirty shirts, five books, four pairs of slippers, two pairs of pants, seven handkerchiefs, a small bottle of eau de Cologne, three socks, a dog skin, a hat and a cap, a pocket barograph, some glasses, and several small articles, the listing of which would exceed the space available here. This list is not interesting as such, but taken as a whole it proves that man is a social animal.

In the evening, while all our boxes were still arrayed on the shore and we did not know where and how we would eat or sleep, the Greenlanders we had hired to transport them stuck their hands into their pockets. They declared that they had enough, and in any case, they always stopped early on Saturdays. In the meantime, one of them took an interest in my rubber boots and, to test the strength of that unfamiliar "metal," stamped on my foot with all his might. At first, I was taken aback by this aggressive behaviour – not at all like the Greenlanders I knew. A lecture in good Bernese (whose guttural sounds, as I knew from experience, would sound most convincing) in conjunction with a twenty-five öre bill saw to it that they would at least help us carry up the sleeping bags and the kitchen boxes. Early the next morning, like little dwarves, they had stacked all the rest of the baggage at our door.

In the meantime, the *Hans Egede* was out in the bay, smoke belching from her smokestack, ready to weigh anchor. We could not let her go without a last salute. We three kayak owners slipped into our boats, the rest into the expedition boat *Ella*,[1] and in parade order, we paddled out and stopped at a respectful distance. Fick, the quiet one, used his lungs to blow his trumpet: *Muss i denn zum Städtle hinaus* (Must I leave this little town) ... The ship answered our salute with flag signals and gun salutes. Both sides waved, and then she turned southward.

The next morning at 10 a.m., the Greenlanders stopped working. They wanted to go to church, they explained, and so we all went along. The little church, with its slender grey wooden columns, was not built for tall people. My diary notes, "Stolberg almost imperilled the chandelier on entering and so did Jost on leaving. The service was supposed to start at 10 a.m. But perhaps the pastor was not ready until 10:30, or we waited until everybody was present. I remember very pleasantly the harmonious disorder among the Sunday-school boys, who sat on the steps at the front: groups totally unaffected and as natural as you find them in Murillo paintings. On the women's side, a little girl sat astride the coal bucket. Her attention was divided between the Lutheran ritual and her bare toes. That didn't bother anyone, nor did the little boy who had installed himself in the choir and gave his talent free rein by enthusiastically imitating the old choirmaster. Our Jost, urged on by his neighbour, bravely sang along from the Greenlandic hymnbook, a bulky book of 450 hymns translated into Eskimo. To judge from samples translated for me, they do not always do justice to the Greenlanders' way of thinking. The painstaking translation into Eskimo certainly testifies to a strong and moving idealism that outweighs any aesthetic or literary considerations.

During the next few days in Holstensborg, we discussed with the pastor and the administrator our plans for the time before continuing our trip north.

---

1 My mother's name (EQS).

The western party, Professor Mercanton, Dr Stolberg and Dr Jost, were to remain in Holstensborg as planned. They would be busy enough setting up all the instruments and starting the atmospheric observations. The four in the traverse group would go inland, forty kilometres up the fjord to Sarfanguak to attend school with David Ohlsen, a Greenlander whom the inspector on North Greenland had recommended the previous year as the man best suited to teaching us the art of handling dog teams.

This was the X, the unknown in my plans. The use of dogs was important, if not indispensable, for crossing the inland ice cap. We had therefore timed our arrival by the first ship of the year that went as far north as Holstensborg, where it would supposedly still be winter at this time. This is also the southernmost region where dogsleds and dog teams are used. Travel to the coastal areas farther north is only possible a month later, and we had to use this short but precious interval to learn how to handle our dogs. This time would have to do, I thought. Some among the experts agreed, but others were sure we could never succeed and that our plan would fail, depending as it did on the use of dogs.

Now the big moment had arrived. On Wednesday, we would ride to Sarfanguak with Dr Petersen from Sukkertoppen, who had kindly timed his official medical trip to coincide with ours. In the meantime, we still had to arrange for some items of equipment to be made in Holstensborg. Above all, there were spare *kamiks* (soft winter boots)[2] for our porters, which had to be sewn from the sealskins I had bought at Sukkertoppen. For this purpose, a whole committee of Greenlander ladies went into action.

Before leaving for Sarfanguak, we also had our dog whips made, which were of very little use to us for the time being. The pastor gave us some theoretical instruction on the side. In North Greenland, everyone has to be able to drive a team. The basic idea seemed to make sense: "If a dog on the right side of the team does not want to pull, do not hit one on the left."

In Sarfanguak, David Ohlsen was unable to start lessons right away. Because of the extremely mild winter, there was not enough snow on the ground, and the ice on the fjord was already breaking up. So it was decided to drive with Ohlsen, his sleds, and dogs to the head of the fjord the next day. Dr Petersen again offered us his motorboat for the ride. Ohlsen did not want to lose any time and gave us his first lesson in the use of the whip that same evening. His knowledge of the Danish language was better than that of the average Greenlander (for whom it is practically nil), and this complemented my fragments of Greenlandic, so that we managed to understand each other quite satisfactorily.

2 In Canada, mukluks (EQS).

The conversation revolved primarily around the Greenland dog whip. This has a handle about fifty centimetres long and a thong of diminishing width six or seven metres long, made of the skin of a special kind of seal. The tip is fashioned from *matak*, the skin of the white whale, which is quite rare. The piece of matak that David Ohlsen gave me as a souvenir I still keep in the empty gold compartment of my wallet. In Greenland, whip thongs are as serious a topic of conversation as ropes are to a Swiss mountaineer.

The Greenlander handles his whip with extraordinary dexterity. He lands a hit where he aims with absolute sureness and a crack as loud as a gunshot. How does he do that? That's his big secret. And even if you did know how, you would be far from being able to do it yourself. We certainly didn't manage it in Sarfanguak, when we posted ourselves at the four corners of David Ohlsen's house and lashed away with our whips as if our lives depended on it. And not without risk. First, you swing the whip backward along its whole length. And then you give it a sudden jerk, which should catapult the whip forward but often wraps it, for quite inexplicable reasons, around the handler's head, leaving blue and red welts. I am sure I received at least as many hits in my practice days as I ever landed on a dog thereafter.

During our first days at the camp, back in the fjord of Sarkardlit, David Ohlsen was rather worried about our progress with the whip. Hössli was the first to show real ability, which he felt he owed to an old family tradition. The course that Ohlsen gave us in the ten days we camped there was very well organized. The order of the day was roughly as follows. Early in the morning, we discussed the misdeeds the dogs had committed during the night. This meant above all their habit of devouring their harnesses and traces. As always, Ohlsen expressed himself carefully but acted decisively. Once again, all the traces had been chewed through. But which dog was the perpetrator? "Hvem spist?" (Who ate them?), Ohlsen asked, casting a critical eye over the team. "Tarsi, perhaps." After that tentative "perhaps," the absolute sureness with which he seized the miscreant by the collar and gave him a purposeful beating was almost ludicrous.

To me and to the others, these beatings seemed at first brutal and repulsive, and we could barely make ourselves take part. But after I saw how the dogs mauled each other until the snow all around was red with blood, I realized that another kind of dog psychology was in order. Of course, there was no question of just blindly hitting a dog. Above all, I remember the remark made by the pastor: If *you* are not able to drive a team well, you must not hit the *dogs*. The better a dog (or a human), the more he resents an unjust whipping. Our brave Tagazer, who once caught an unmerited punishment from Ohlsen, showed his moral indignation all through the following day. When I made a similar mistake much later with our lead dog, Mons, an even better dog of superior character, Mons turned away full of contempt as if to say, "What a dolt." Ohlsen taught us to tie up the snouts of dogs who had the bad habit of chewing up the harnesses during the night. And, if there were relapses, step 2 was applied: the incorrigible one had a string tied right through his mouth.

From checking the dog harnesses, we proceeded logically to their repair. Since I am not as fortunate as my companions in sleeping soundly, I was the first to be approached by Ohlsen with the early-morning mending chores. This was not really to my taste. So one day I explained to my pitiless instructor: "There in the tent is one, the Nakorsak (the doctor, as Hössli was affectionately known), who would be really eager to mend harnesses too, if only he had a chance. Nothing he'd rather do." Ohlsen did not need to be told twice, and from then on he burdened the unsuspecting Nakorsak with dog harnesses. This worthy took it in good spirit, and the special facility he soon acquired was to be of great importance at a difficult moment on the ice cap.

To drive a team, one has to come to an understanding with the animals about the meaning of *left* and *right*, *stop* and *stand still*, *slow* and *fast*. In this entente, it must be made quite clear, either with the whip or by friendly persuasion, that the driver is the boss, the absolute authority. But don't we sometimes have to admit that the little ones go their own way? After several practice rides on two frozen mountain lakes, where we had to drive thirty kilometres by ourselves, the preliminary course was passed.

Then came the more difficult descent of a steep slope, which Ohlsen considered most important in view of the eastern slopes of the ice cap, which he imagined were extremely steep. My diary, written right after work with blue, cold fingers says: "Today we got to the main part, working the sleds down very steep slopes with the dogs behind the sleds to do the braking with their paws. The word to the dogs is *Imatsiak, imatsiak* (slow, slow). Hössli and I are under Ohlsen's supervision, Fick and Gaule under his helper's, Setti Kleist. You stand behind the loaded sled, one hand on the back rail. The other one swings the whip in a high arc, left and right, without stopping, to keep the dogs back. The dogs' eight traces lead somehow between your legs. You have to get to grips with this. If the dogs are well trained, they advance slowly, braking continuously. If the dogs and their master are incompetent, you end up as a small avalanche of humans and dogs."

In between the sledging exercises, Fick went hunting for us. Usually one finds only ptarmigan – not much of an honour for the hunter, as ptarmigan are naive, even stupid. But when Fick outwitted a wily snow hare, the largest animal one finds in this barren region, Ohlsen's respect grew, and he advised me to make "Pick" our hunter if we had to live off the land on the east coast.

On the aforementioned lake, we also tried out our sledge sailing rig and the sledge meter, a wheel with a counter that would measure the distance we had run on the ice cap.

On 9 May, we graduated from David Ohlsen's school, *Nu tamase ajungilak* (Now everything is working fine), provided, though, that we took an additional course in mending kamiks with his wife, for he was convinced that a lack of knowledge in such matters had led to the loss of Mylius-Erichsen.[3]

It would have been an edifying sight to see the eastern party two days later, sitting at the feet of the wise Ania Ohlsen, diligently mending kamiks, pulling the three-sided needle with their teeth through the leather. Her amiable daughters Agatha and Igner helped or entertained us with their harmonica playing, a talent possessed by David Ohlsen too. He even owned a small organ. The first thing he played out of an old English hymnbook was *Integer vitae*! And Mrs Ohlsen knew the Greenlandic words for it.

The repertoire of an old phonograph, which Ohlsen had once received from an official who was returning to Europe, was rather out of character, though. From among the dusty rolls, Ohlsen picked a potpourri from the operetta *Taxicab*. Very appropriate! But I also found *Connais tu le pays ou fleurit l'oranger*? In the middle of it, the phonograph gave up with a loud outcry. And rightly so. The winds howling around the house did not come from the "blue Mediterranean." And what greeted us outside on the way to our hut prompted Hössli's grim variation:

> Kennst du das Land wo Schweinehunde steh'n,
> wo knietief man durch Dreck und Mist nach Haus muss geh 'n … ?[4]

And indeed, the surroundings of a Greenland house in the rain were not for delicate noses and fine ladies' boots. After Ohlsen's twelve originally snow-white dogs had been fighting in the mud – several times a day, sending up a hellish racket – Hössli's imprecations started to sound almost tame in comparison.

We had a chance to obtain quite a number of human footprints, as valuable material for anthropological studies. By offering a big coffee party, we were finally

3 Ludwig Mylius-Erichsen (1872–1907), a Danish explorer and journalist, led two expeditions to Greenland. A lack of suitable footwear for hunting in the summer months may have led to his death on the second expedition.

4 Do you know the country where the scumdogs roam, / where you needs must walk knee-deep through dirt and mire just to get home?

able to convince even the ladies of the village to participate. Only the Ohlsens' social position in the village kept them from taking part with the common people. But actually, I have the feeling that they would really have liked to lend their dainty footprints for preservation in the name of science.

By now we had mended every possible piece of torn kamik in the Ohlsen family, to Mrs Ohlsen's great amusement. We had also started to eat a lot of pemmican, as our other supplies were running low. And still the inclement weather delayed our return to Holstensborg. When we asked David Ohlsen, he would look west and reply laconically, "Anore nalagak": the storm is master. Finally the storm let up, and we returned by rowboat to Holstensborg in bitter cold, happy to replace a Greenlander at the oars from time to time just to keep warm. Again and again, we watched Setti Kleist with admiration as he fought storm and waves with untiring skill in his iced-up kayak beside us. (A year later, I received the sad news from David Ohlsen in his laconic style that "Seth Kleist perished in his kayak.") We reached the harbour at Holstensborg just before it froze over, an unheard-of occurrence in the second half of May.

Before travelling on northward, we filled the time in Holstensborg by practising some more with the dogs, this time with fully loaded sleds. We also divided the food into rations and prepared everything for the trip on the ice cap. This included painting all the leather and wooden parts with tar, as the dogs dislike its taste so much that sometimes they will refrain from chewing it.

While we had the time to train for several hours every day on short ski trips, we had to abandon the idea of any larger excursions, especially of climbing the Kjäringhetten, as the work plan just did not allow it. For all of us, this was a time of strenuous activities, which I shall describe briefly. On our return to Holstensborg, we found our friends from the western party working at full tilt. Mercanton was busy calibrating his instruments. He was also trying to receive wireless signals from the Eiffel Tower. Stolberg and Jost shared the meteorological observations, and now and then had to hunt for the dogs who had run away with thermometers in their mouths. They had started the atmospheric measurements, especially the ones with the weather balloons. Several trials with kites and tethered balloons gave rather interesting results. The southeast wind, often present at the height of a few hundred metres, is in reality a dry foehn wind. Unfortunately, our equipment suffered quite a bit in these bad weather experiments. Jost was also an excellent colour photographer, whose most appreciative subjects were the Holstensborg beauties in their flamboyant costumes.

Hössli did double duty as quartermaster and doctor, which kept him very busy. A bad influenza epidemic had broken out in Holstensborg, sparing nobody and proving quite dangerous for the Greenlanders. Hössli treated countless numbers of patients. Although popular myth sometimes unjustly called him the "noble medic," he didn't hesitate to crawl into the dirtiest hut. His Danish colleagues in Sukkertoppen and the administrator had asked him to take on the medical supervision of the small but well-equipped hospital. He was even called to neighbouring villages, and in one case did a successful abdominal operation on a critically ill patient in a Greenlander's hut. Fick was Hössli's assistant in non-medical jobs and head of the technical section. We very much appreciated his dexterity and readiness to help at all times. Gaule, our keen-witted physicist, sometimes libellously slurred as materialistic, looked after preparations for the atmospheric electrical measurements and above all the determination of astronomical time, in order to check our chronometers. This was most important, because on the ice cap we would base all our longitude calculations on their accuracy. At first, there were strange contradictions in the Holstensborg observations, until we realized that the town's latitude on the nautical charts was not quite accurate.

We often worked late into the night to finish the day's program, and we organized the next day's work at our daily meetings. These regular conferences ensured that we all knew each other's work and that there would not be any of the information-hoarding that so often interferes with the work of scientists who work in close proximity.

Despite the weeks of hard work, there were some joyous feasts, which, although modest, were happy occasions for us and for our guests. First, there were the birthdays of all the members of the expedition. By special edict, we had agreed to celebrate them all sometime during the expedition. According to this rule, Stolberg's and Hössli's fell on 30 April, Mercanton got 16 May, and Jost picked 30 May because it was his name-day. But for some reason I never thought of "Wilhelm" but rather of "Justus," and my clever speech was accordingly based on Saint Justus. Everybody liked it, but the benevolent critics reminded me that really it was Wilhelm's day.

Later, when the little steamer *Fox* and the sailboat *Thorwaldsen* were in the harbour at the same time – a considerable naval concentration for Greenland – we boldly invited the ships' officers together with the prominent people of the town for an expedition tea. We set up a table from two doors taken off their hinges, made chairs from pemmican boxes, and borrowed cups from Mr Thron. Our guests graciously appreciated our menu, especially the Swiss canned foods, but the rock-hard rye bread intended for the ice cap, which we had included to round out the presentation, was judged quite harshly.

The high point of our social life was the invitation to dinner from David Ohlsen and his family, who were visiting Holstensborg from Sarfanguak. The

Ohlsens conducted themselves like country squires. While the Holstensborg youth happily danced with the sailors until closing time, the Ohlsens would usually dance once or twice and then retire.

Language posed some problems at our party, and we tried to overcome the gaps in verbal communication with friendliness, offering our delicacies with the typical question: "Ajungila?" (Is it good?) This was answered by "Ap, mamakrak." (Yes, it tastes very good.) Such was the modesty of our conversational elements. But things improved when we pushed the "furniture" of the dining room aside and started the *soirée dansante*. The Ohlsens asked if they could invite some cousins, and soon there were more social engagements, as my diary notes:

"Saturday, about 10 or 12 p.m., how should I know? I only have my chronometer set on Greenwich Time with me, and anyway, day and night are nearly the same. Outside there is a permanent sunset. Boundless quiet and clarity lie over the sea and the snow-capped rocks. And in here, we are having a big dance party. It started with twelve but now we have over fifty people. And although I write in an adjoining room, my pen shakes as if during a continuous earthquake."

Incidentally, that night there was a small altercation with officialdom in the person of the Greenlander who wanted us to respect the closing hour, 10 p.m., because he obviously didn't consider this to be any longer a closed party. However, the public merrymaking, as it had actually turned out to be, ended in perfect harmony when I suggested we finish up with a cup of coffee. The people and the police could agree on that.

On the whole, we were more often guests than hosts in Holstensborg. Pastor Friedrichsen, a widower at the time, kindly invited us to share his delicious reindeer roast. And quite often some of us would sit together for a long evening at the home of Administrator Thron, another widower.

On the *Fox*, they had been talking mysteriously for a while now about a *skovtour* – a forest party – on Whitsunday. Even in Greenland, the forest-loving Danes must have their excursion into the forest, and a fertile imagination should have no difficulty in conjuring up a forest where the dwarf willows try to raise themselves up in a sunny corner behind some rocks. In such a forest, the kind people from the *Fox* erected a Whitsun tent and offered an inviting choice of edible and potable treats. To round off the event, rowing boats and sailing boats raced each other back to the ship. Sadly, this was the only part of this party I saw. Influenza kept me away, and Fick kindly kept me company.

CHAPTER 5
NORTHWARD WITH THE *FOX*

The old *Fox* was ready, all her winter damage made good. After a snowstorm had held us up for several days, we left Holstensborg a wintrier place on 1 June than we had found it in April. We said warm goodbyes to all, to the Greenlanders, to the ever-helpful Pastor Friedrichsen, and to Administrator Thron, who had always been ready to assist when we needed him.

To our astonishment, the Swiss flag was hoisted to the top of the mast as soon as we were under way, and it remained there as long as we were on board the *Fox*. This had been Captain Stocklund's idea, and he had made the flag himself, together with his brother, the first mate. There was not much room on the *Fox*. Most of us slept on deck and, when it rained, on the floor of the large lifeboat. But what marvellous days we spent with the kind crew on the *Fox*! We all treasure the memory of these days with a special warmth, partly because the *Fox* so cunningly kept to a channel inside the islands, where the effects of heavy seas could not reach us. On the other hand, there were other hazards to be met. By no means all the shoals and reefs in this maze of islands are known and marked on the charts. So the *Fox* ran aground every now and then and had to sit there until the next high tide floated her again. This happened on the way from Holstensborg to Agto when we sailed into a fog bank. Everybody calmly accepted the delay of twenty-four hours. We knew that the *Fox*'s sturdy planks of doubled oak were made to withstand hidden reefs. When the fog lifted for a while over a neighbouring island, we organized an outing in order to determine our latitude. After the ship was sufficiently lightened (because of the extra meals eaten, the engineer claimed), she straightened up again, and we reached Agto without further mishaps.

On arrival, one of the first things to be done was to organize a kayak courier to Egedesminde to order dog food. We hadn't been able to find any in Holstensborg, and we feared that it might also be scarce further north before the *angmagsettes* (capelins)[1] run in June. But I certainly could not wait that long on the coast, nor could we open the pemmican supply before reaching the ice cap. Twice I had sent kayak couriers northwards from Holstensborg, but without success. Storms and ice had forced them to turn back.

On our initial night in Agto we saw the midnight sun for the first time. For hours, the icebergs lay bathed in a wonderful yellow-red and bluish light. The colours were rather emphatic, not glaring but glowingly warm.

While I acted as Hössli's interpreter on his rounds of the sick Greenlanders, guided by the eldest of the Danish official's six girls, Fick entertained the healthy. His reputation as a musician had preceded him, and he earned considerable applause with a trumpet concert. Our kayak fleet, now numbering six boats and boatmen, who were able to go on extended trips, was duly admired. But on one occasion, Fick and Gaule, whose homemade kayaks had earned special appreciation from the locals everywhere, narrowly missed a real hazard. An overhanging iceberg they had just passed broke in two. A few seconds earlier, and they would have been buried in ice rubble.

We reached Egedesminde on the evening of 4 June. Five large wooden houses standing in a row almost made it look like a town. Samuelsen, who was to supply our dogs, had sent a message to Egedesminde the previous year, but it had never arrived. However, dog food was available, and Ollrich, the commercial assistant, agreed to sell us his beautiful dog team. As is often the case, he kept it on an uninhabited island for the summer.

In Egedesminde, we also made a rapid decision to have some wooden backpacks made for the transport over the rock zone later on. I also bought green, red, and blue ribbons so that we could tell our dog teams apart.

The *Fox* was to leave Egedesminde early on 7 June. The day before, the ship's carpenter had built a large pen on one side of the deck for the future dog pack, and the first team, Ollrich's nine, were about to be brought on board early in the morning. It was a real Egedesminde dawn, sad, grey, and foggy. The expedition crew, just back from a birthday dance in honour of a pretty Danish colonist, was

---

1 The capelin (or caplin) is a small forage fish of the smelt family found in Arctic waters. In Greenland at this time, the catch was used for dog food.

still fast asleep. It fell to me to fetch and welcome on board our worthy future companions for the ice cap. In the process, we had to sunder close family ties. Mons, our lead dog (here usually called *Nalagak,* or "Sir"), a head taller than the rest, left an extended family behind, particularly two male puppies who ran up and down on the shore yelping wretchedly, while their composed and noble sire was led off to the ship and a great new destiny.

The emotional attachments of Greenland dogs reach far beyond narrow family ties. Nobody who has experience with Greenland dogs will forget this basic fact of Greenland dogs' lives. When the *Fox* weighed anchor and we moved away from the land, waving goodbye, the dogs realized that the time for an appropriate performance had come. Silke started it, the others joined in, and the nine-fold unison swelled till it drowned out the ship's whistle. It soon found a living echo onshore until the howling of a hundred Egedesminde dogs soared up to heaven like a fiery flame.

First, *Fox* set course for Akugdlit, a small settlement in the southeast bay. We had arranged with the administration that we would get our remaining dog teams there. Their supplier, Samuelsen, an old acquaintance of Stolberg's, was to be the leader of the Greenlanders hired as porters to help us as far as the ice cap. In the meantime, the kayak courier, who had returned the night before, told us that Samuelsen did have dogs, but that he was ill and in no condition to accompany us to the ice cap. This was bad news indeed. All my efforts to find a replacement in Egedesmine, even with Mr Ollrich's help, remained unsuccessful.

For a while, we had an old acquaintance in tow, the ketch *Louise.* Three years ago, we had watched her sail off, eager to catch walrus. But it turned out that the wind died every time walrus were around and when the wind revived, the walrus disappeared. There really seemed to be no way to get near them, and so the *Louise* had reverted to transporting blubber oil. To compensate for the demotion, she had received a beautiful new coat of green and yellow paint, just as people in our neighbouring countries sometimes receive titles and medals.

Approaching Akugdlit, we left the damp fog further and further behind us. As we came near the islands, we were astonished to see the sunlight showing up green patches amidst the red-brown heather. In the more sheltered bay where the settlement lies, there were real little meadows. The close proximity of the mainland and the dry offshore winds, which blow almost constantly, make a striking difference to the bleak terrain at Egedesminde. The Greenlanders at Akugdlit were greatly astonished to see a proud ship like the *Fox* anchor for the first time in their harbour, and they greeted us from afar in their friendly manner.

Before we could start our dog trading, there were several patients for Dr Hössli, since it was already known that we had a doctor among us. The doctor in Jakobshavn was on leave, and his substitute had not made a visit all winter, probably because it had not been cold enough for the sea ice to form. Some people were suffering from influenza. One man had a critical ear infection. Because we planned to be here only for a short while, Hössli regretfully could not risk the necessary surgical intervention, a type of operation that he later successfully performed in East Greenland. As I had done previously and would later in similar situations, my job was to translate. There is an optimistic saying that wisdom comes with the position. But in this case, it wasn't so. We tried very hard indeed, which was better than nothing, and Hössli worked quite successfully despite the difficulties.

However, the dog trade that followed was a dark chapter – not for us, but for the dogs.

The Samuelsen team had been ordered for the expedition the previous fall and, in our imagination, we had endowed it with a supernatural qualities. But no! Were these jaundiced creatures supposed to be the vaunted Samuelsen team? They were thin curs. Our faces grew longer and longer as they were introduced one by one. Had we not been able to compare them with the beautiful Egedesminde team, we might have shown more confidence in these yellow mutts. Was it for these starved creatures that the *Fox* had detoured to Akugdlit? On the other hand, could I be certain of getting better dogs – or any dogs at all – in Jakobshavn? What do Central Europeans know of the deep secrets of dog lore in North Greenland? Could it be that the smaller and scrawnier the dogs, the better they pull?

In any case, faced with our unconcealed doubts, the Akugdlit Greenlanders all closed ranks and supported this rather paradoxical thesis. As Schopenhauer said, "For all these centuries, truth has had to blush because it is paradoxical." Couldn't this also be true for Samuelsen's dogs? So I purchased them in good faith, somewhat comforted by the fact that I could also get a second team that might look less ridiculous. Not without difficulty, the sixteen dogs were put into a boat and brought on board the ship, where they were greeted by the incumbents with bared teeth. In a Greenlandic dog, this looks off-putting, not to say downright repulsive. No matter how pleasant and trustworthy the animal sometimes seemed to be, now only the wild beast remained – a wolf.

But soon the dogs agreed to a truce. As the *Fox* steamed out into the open water, heading northward toward Jakobshavn, they realized they were all fellow sufferers, and they soon joined together in howling. From time to time, one of them would rear up against the wall and sniff around. But there was nothing doing and no hope, nothing but water as far as a short-sighted dog's eye could see.

For us who were not so cooped up and could see further out, the journey was more agreeable. As the coast was never more than four to five kilometres away, we could observe the many peculiarities of the coastal formation. There were high shoreline terraces along the mountainsides and also the enormous gravel terraces of some earlier glaciation, lifted above sea level in an area where a side arm of what is now the Jakobshavn glacier had once reached the sea. At times, we could even see the inland ice cap above the fjord and the mountains of Orpiksuit, looking like a thin flat layer of mist above the coastal range. On seeing our old friend and adversary again, Stolberg and I obviously felt quite different emotions from those of the others They had yet to experience the reality portended by this delicate thin grey zone within the white band, what detours it implied and what labours, and how unattainable, how invincible this fine horizontal line would be, forever receding into the distance.

The sun stood low on the northern horizon as we approached the Jakobshavn glacier. Many would have given a fortune to join us for the passage between these walls of ice. For hours, we had on our right, near the fjord's mouth, a wall of icebergs that had been shoved out onto a shoal by the ice masses thrusting from behind. To our left, a huge flotilla of icebergs had regained their freedom and were now drifting toward a gentle dissolution in milder latitudes.

It would be a hopeless task to paint this mood, to string words together to describe these forms and colours. I might try to paint them with a brush, or even to capture them with a cinematograph. But this latest invention seems to me an underhand, roundabout way of recording things, one that our dishonest culture has spawned in order to create what, at best, is an illusion. We felt at the time that this gigantic experience was inalienably ours. Prattle about it, promote it as we will, we can convey to others but a feeble gleam, and the fire remains ours alone. The real experience cannot be recreated, here or elsewhere.

Dusk was falling when we sailed into Jakobshavn. Between the colony's well-built houses, the Greenlanders stood in picturesque groups on the boulders and waved to the year's first ship. Among them, we could distinguish a differently clad group of people: the Danish colonists. But it was their European summer hats that really astonished us. These meant that it was officially summer here. And barely a week ago in Holstensborg, three hundred kilometres to the south, we had been mired in deep snow. But, like happiness itself, the fleeting Greenlandic summer must be snatched while it is present.

Having already heard that a Swiss expedition planned to cross the ice cap, the Jakobshavn Danes were ready and waiting with their doubts. No sooner were they on board than they aimed a volley of questions at me. Some of these queries implied that they felt we Swiss were possessed of rather less than average reasoning power. I think I answered with a reasonable degree of patience, given my temperament, until some self-appointed expert asked what we would do if we reached the east coast a hundred kilometres north or south of Angmagssalik. The answer was brief: that was what our sextant was for, and now it would be better not to get lost on the way to bed.

"Bed" was too proud a word for my sleeping place on the *Fox*. As we had a sudden foehn wind and were expecting rain, the captain graciously put the equipment room at my disposal. The bench was unquestionably too narrow to sleep on, but then the space beside it was also too narrow to fall into. So I found a state of unstable equilibrium, which worked well enough.

On arrival in the evening, we had arranged to meet the next day with Administrator Ohlsen, Pastor Osterman, the commercial assistant Krogh, and the captain of the *Fox* in order to choose our landing site, hire a crew of Greenlanders, and make up the number of dogs in our pack. We are deeply indebted to these gentlemen for their unstinting concern for us, and the help they afforded the expedition in word and deed.

We found right from the beginning of our discussion that we had to drop our plan to reach the ice cap from the Pakitsok Fjord to the north of Jakobshavn. This location had initially looked promising to us because Peary had considered it in his 1883 attempt as the shortest and easiest access route, and it is relatively close to Jakobshavn. As it turned out, however, an underwater bar at the mouth of the fjord meant the depth was too shallow for the *Fox* to sail over, even at high tide. It would take too much time to load our gear into boats at this place and transport it the considerable distance to the head of the fjord. And besides, the advantage of having the *Fox* at our disposal would have been lost.

Luckily, while making arrangements the previous year, it had already occurred to me that we might not find a passage up to the ice cap either at Orpiksuit or Pakitsok. I had then agreed with the inspector of North Greenland that, in advance of our arrival, two Greenlanders would go out in spring and explore a third region that looked promising, a rocky area adjacent to the ice cap farther north, at the head of the Ata Sound, south of the Torsukatak glacier. This reconnaissance had been organized by Mr Ohlsen. But at the moment, we did not know what they had found, as the Greenlanders who lived farther north were only expected to report in upon the *Fox*'s arrival, and she had reached Jakobshavn three days ahead of schedule.

We decided not to lose any time waiting around and instead to steam up Ata Sound the next day and look for the two kayakers. But first we would hire a crew of Greenlanders as helpers.

Although Jakobshavn, with about four hundred inhabitants, is quite a big place for Greenland, it was difficult to find a dozen men for our transport from the shore to the rim of the ice cap. It proved even more difficult, almost impossible, to hire Greenlanders willing to accompany us for the first stage on the ice cap itself. I have to thank the diligence of the pastor, who had the unconditional trust of his parishioners, that by the end of the day I had my crew. The reason for these difficulties is that what the Greenlander calls "work" is for him a most unpleasant thing. Yet to paddle a kayak for the longest distances to hunt seal or to march long distances over hills and through valleys with heavy loads to hunt reindeer is not considered "work."

As a result, there was much calculating and moaning, accompanied by many an "ajorpok" and "ajornakrak" (it's no good, it does not work anymore) about activities such as lugging rocks, coal, and boxes that, in a Greenlander's mind, are women's work, Even the most modest effort prompted the remark "mange arbejd" (lots of work). Greenlanders even resort to using the Danish words to make it clear how shameful such a request was. In our case, an added complication was that the angmagsettes fish run was expected any day soon, when capable people could earn handsomely even without the shame of working. It was impossible to retain the most able men for the ice cap, because this would have taken too much of their time.

We still had to make up our dog teams and, if possible, improve them. We were fortunate to have the support of the commercial assistant Krogh, whom we knew to be a dog expert. I brought forward our pack of dogs, and, in general, his remarks were positive. So I was most anxious to hear his opinion on Samuelsen's yellow ones. His unconcealed mirth proved that, in this case, the concept of the "paradoxical truth" wouldn't apply. He found that some of them really were too small and scrawny, and generously offered to exchange them – for a small consideration – for good sledge dogs.

While Hössli and I attended to this business in Jakobshavn, Mercanton, Stolberg, and Jost had gone overland to the surrounding hills to take photographs and make measurements of the icebergs at the fjord's mouth. Gaule, who had become a good astronomical observer and would take a lot of work off my shoulders, worked with Fick on measuring the sun's position with the sextant to determine the local time and the accuracy of the chronometers. I planned to measure the longitude during the ice cap crossing in relation to Jakobshavn, for which the absolute longitude was the most accurately measured of any place on the west coast. These observations had been made by Ohlsen, the colonial administrator, who is not only a businessman but also an observant and competent astronomer. He had had the dedication to carry out the celestial observations that were now such a great boon to us. Ohlsen showed us his small observatory, as proud of it as Mrs Ohlsen was of her greenhouse, which would have qualified her as the Semiramis of the North had not Mrs Osterman and her rose garden laid equal claim to the title.

In addition to its scientific and aesthetic attractions, Jakobshavn also takes pride in some very practical ones, the latest being the telephone wire that runs from house to house in the colony. We were astonished to see a long row of poles leading over a high hill to the manse, a fair distance away. On the long winter evenings, when snow and cold keep the ladies at home, there is probably many a conversation that goes on far longer than would be permitted by European protocols. What a fortunate land: a telephone free both of charge and of an officiously interrupting switchboard operator!

Alas, every paradise must be lost, and so we had to leave this one in North Greenland. Early on Sunday, 10 June, the steam whistle summoned us all aboard the *Fox*, which for the next few days would now serve exclusively as our expedition ship. Besides the crew of Greenlanders, there was also Pastor Osterman, who in so many instances was our valuable interpreter and advisor, and Mr Lindow, a lawyer and a pleasant companion.

During the last few days, I had worked so far into the night that I was glad to lie down for a while to sleep on deck in the sun.

We had sailed a good distance into Ata Sound when I was wakened and told that we had met a man in a kayak who knew that the two Greenlanders we wanted to meet were on shore in Roede Bay. We had passed this point a while ago. Having no choice but to turn back, we met the two as they returned from a white whale hunt. We were eager to hear what they knew about the area around the Eqip Sermia, and the report sounded quite favourable. They said that access to the ice cap was possible for porters, and that the rim of the ice was flat at that spot. The older of the two men wanted to go home, but the younger one, Vitus from Arsivik, agreed to accompany us through the rocks and onto the ice cap for five days. He would be the leader of the Greenlanders. For the time being, he acted as the ship's pilot.

But we did not sail directly to the bay of the Eqip Sermia, where we were to land. First we went to Ata, a small settlement on the west side of the sound on Arveprinzens Island, where we wanted to pick up two large Greenland dog sledges. Vitus had also mentioned that the route to the ice cap goes across a heath for a stretch, and that the dogs should certainly be able to pull light loads on the Greenland sledges over this passage.

After we left Ata, making our way eastward between isolated icebergs, a spectacular view opened up over the wide northern bay of the sound. To the north glittered the densely packed icebergs of the Torsukatak glacier, against the backdrop of the blue hills on the great Nugsuak Peninsula. To the northeast and east towered three massive dark rock pillars flanking the ice cap, which pushed in two wide fronts right down to the bay. Our trail would lead over the southernmost of these rock massifs, which is connected to the vast terrains north of the Pakitsok Fjord. The *Fox* now steered through the still blue waters to the southeast corner of the bay.

But the silence was not to endure much longer up here. A joyous yodeller announced to this frozen world that life was now arriving – in the shape of a Swiss expedition. Never had the Greenlanders heard such sounds, and their "amalu" (encore!) showed how much they appreciated it. Jost and Hössli, our splendid Swiss boys, kept on yodelling so that even the rocks, which would normally only answer to the roar of storms or the growling of icebergs, seemed happy to re-echo these alien sounds.

CHAPTER 6
CROSSING THE ROCK BORDER

In the evening the *Fox* dropped anchor in the lee of a small peninsula, although the area where Vitus thought we should land was a whole hour's rowing further to the east. But that spot was so close to the wall of the Eqip Sermia glacier that the captain had misgivings about staying there for the night. And I did not want to start unloading our equipment without checking myself, together with Vitus, that his description of the route to the ice cap was correct, especially since he said that we would need a whole day to go there and back. The map indicated a distance of only four kilometres and a difference in altitude of four hundred metres. We had to leave immediately in order to return as soon as possible, since the ship could not sail into the inner bay without Vitus on board as pilot. So Jost and I got ready to row into the bay in the expedition boat *Ella*. But the *Ella* had sat on deck in the sun for so long that fountains of water sprayed through all the joints between the boards. I was reminded of the Grandes Eaux at Versailles. We hurriedly climbed into another boat.

No longer blue, the water here was clouded for quite a distance by the glacier streams, green at first and then milkily opaque. Moraines stretched along the shore, indicating that the glacier had been much wider in relatively recent times.

From the shore, our route crossed rhododendron bushes in bloom. Between them willows nestled close to rock boulders, a familiar and, to our increasingly modest expectations, quite lush vegetation. From there we climbed more steeply up the valley along a stream that descended in numerous small waterfalls from a lake on the high plateau. This lake was still half-covered in winter ice no longer strong enough to bear us. It barred our direct access to the ice cap that seemed so near behind a gneiss ridge, forcing us to make a wide detour.

After we had reached almost the height of the ice, I understood why Vitus kept murmuring in a critical tone, "Korok ajorpok" (No good). We had to descend into the valley again and climb steeply round on the other side. This time the final slope led over snowfields and rounded ridges toward the ice cap. We knew we were close by the strong southeast wind that blows incessantly, forcing the last few blades of grass to shelter in timid rakes behind stones. The wind had even harried these pebbles into orderly rows.

Up there we were glad to turn our backs for a moment against the powerful wind and look back over the high plateau we had just crossed before covering the last stretch to the ice. However remarkable this surface was with its numerous lakes, streams, waterfalls, and rock ridges, the sight made me uncomfortable. Indeed, I felt an absolute revulsion for this piece of earth, fated as it was to eternal sterility and incapable even of hiding this grim destiny. It was with true relief that I later set foot onto the ice cap. Strange as it may seem, the cold ice felt neither sterile nor forbidding to me. In fact, it seemed quite congenial.

As far as we could see, the ice cap was rimmed by a huge moraine whose crest towered about fifty metres over the rocky foreland. The drop from the crest was quite steep but fortunately still covered by a snowpack almost a metre deep. We also found a place where the snow slope continued through a notch in the wall of the moraine all the way to the slope of solid ice, which rose in an easterly direction to the horizon. Thus, an uninterrupted path for the sleds was assured, right from the edge of the ice.

We continued on for about a kilometre and found that the ice rose in a sequence of moderate steps and almost flat areas toward the east. As far as we could judge, it should not pose any great difficulty to us. The snow, it is true, had disappeared everywhere, but the erosion of the solid ice by small runnels of meltwater had only just started. These rivulets were small, incised as yet to only a hand's depth. There were numerous cryoconite holes, still not very deep and partly frozen over.[1]

---

1 On his journeys to Greenland in 1867 and 1883, the Finnish-Swedish explorer Baron Adolf Erik Nordenskjöld noted frequent hollows of meltwater in the ice cap. He wrote several papers on the origin of "kryokonite," as he termed the mineral deposits that collected at the bottom of such hollows. Chemical analysis later proved that the deposits came from coal dust residues blown in from the chimneys of Europe and North America.

On the whole, the situation in the rim zone was as I had expected for mid-June, based on my experience in the Karajak region. This much was certain. We could not have found a more favourable place as our starting point for crossing the ice cap. It is true that the distance from the sea, according to the Goerz rangefinder binoculars, which had so far served us well, was double that given on the map. And the altitude of the ice rim was quite a bit higher; we reckoned about six hundred metres.

Even if the transport to the rim was going to be more laborious and time-consuming than expected, the obstacles in the border zone of the ice would be smaller because of the higher starting point.

On our return trip, we put up a pole with the Swiss flag at the ice rim to serve as a markers for the others, who would be coming later. We also cached the instruments and some food supplies we had with us, just in case. Among these was honey, of which we had plenty in our stores, a much-appreciated gift from my theologian brother, who of course knew about the honey experts Solomon and Jonathan before the modern science of physiology recognized the value of sugar for improved athletic performance. At that moment, it must have been obvious that I was enthused by the honey, for I did my best to explain its origin and husbandry to the Greenlanders Vitus and Anton, who also approved the product with many a "Mamakrak" (Very good). In my analogy, I used Greenlandic mosquitoes instead of bees, with dubious success. Usually I envied Gaule for his enthusiasm and confidence when he dared to undertake such explanations. He never shrank from any challenge, whether in translating a Busch verse or telling the story of the runner from Uri.

As we reached the heath on our way back to the sea, the first mosquitoes came humming toward us, and with each step they became more numerous. That was a bad omen for the coming transport. The Greenlander rowers slept beside the boat with their heads tightly wrapped. No sooner had we shaken them awake and pulled the boat into the water than we ourselves fell asleep. The only way for us to stay awake was to row too. This had been another typical Greenlandic twenty-four-hour day.

It was Monday morning, 11 June, when Jost and I and the two Greenlanders returned to the ship. There was no sleep for me for the time being, because the unloading and overland transport first had to be organized. A strong foehn wind made the work more difficult, but at least it kept the mosquitoes away on the first day.

Above all, the thirty dogs had to be brought onshore. They were to be used to pull the sleds over the heath. While unloading, Fick had the misfortune to fall into the ship's hold and bruise his hip quite badly. Gaule, too, felt unwell.

A small injury on his forehead had somehow become infected, but in the evening he marched off to the ice cap with Mercanton, who wanted to check how the area could be used as a starting point for his future work. In the meantime, everybody else was busy with the transport under Hössli's leadership.

As I recall, it was cruel drudgery for man and beast to drag the sleds over the plants on the shore. This method was of doubtful value, and it most certainly ruined our dog harnesses. We saw with misgivings that the Greenlanders treated our dogs and our material quite carelessly. The harnesses that were not torn up then were lost the following week, when the dogs were tied up on the beach in the care of a Greenlander.

The next two days, or rather nights, were used for transport. During the day, work was almost impossible because of the mosquitoes. We had to use our time well: our best porters were going to leave us on Wednesday on the *Fox* because they did not want to miss the big event of the year, the angmagsettes fishery. Through the intermediary Pastor Osterman in Jakobshavn, who sent a kayak messenger to the settlements of Ata and Arsivik, I had been able to find three more porters who, however, did not express great joy at exchanging the proud twin paddle for a backpack.

The captain had recorded the majestic yet idyllic landing bay between the rocky shore and the ice wall of the Eqip Sermia as "Quervainshavn" in his ship's log and had the name painted on a rock in huge letters in the Swiss colours, red and white. He had even, I heard, helped paint them himself. It was obvious that such cordiality, not to mention the Swiss flag flying from the masthead, imposed a certain obligation on us. In my short farewell speech in Danish, I said that there was now no way out of "Quervainshavn" except to the east.

The farewell was particularly warm, and some of the ship's crew could not hide their emotions. In their hearts, they doubted that we would be successful. The little cabin boy Julius had tears running down his cheeks. After three thundering cheers from the crew assembled at the stern, the *Fox* was soon lost to view in the distance, and only a dark streak of smoke floated above the icebergs.

This was the last voyage of this ship, which had earned its renown after Franklin's disappearance. Shortly afterwards, she foundered off Agto.[2]

We were too tired to gaze after the *Fox* for long. Above all, we were looking for rest in our sleeping bags, as far as mosquito bites and howling dogs would permit. I even tried to refresh myself with a little sea bath, though it proved to be all too fresh in the glacier's immediate vicinity.

---

2 *Fox* was the ship that Lady Franklin sent to search for Franklin's expedition (EQS).

When I rejoined my companions in the evening, I realized that the atmosphere was less than exuberant. They had the impression that the remaining porters wanted to walk out as well. Hössli had heard them mutter "Atamut" and "Arvisimut." And *-mut*, the locative ending in reply to the question "where to?" was for us a doleful suffix.

Indeed, some of the porters came with very definite reasons why they had to leave immediately. One had weak eyes and had lost his protective goggles, the second had bad lungs, the third an aching leg. What could we do at such a juncture if we did not want to appear as oppressors of humanity? But *praesente medico nihil nocet* (nothing bad can happen in the presence of a doctor). What luck! We had our Dr Hössli, MD. I could tell the Greenlanders how fortunate they were, because their maladies could not be better cared for than in the presence of our Nakorsak, who would now examine them right away. Which he did. Hössli gave the first one goggles out of our supplies, dark as night. No way out now! The second one was made to understand that his alleged ailment was caused solely by excessive tobacco-chewing. He had to swallow the bitter truth instead of the tobacco and go on carrying his burden. The third one was given the needed treatment by scalpel and was relegated to quiet duties or guarding the dogs while he recuperated.

In order to consolidate our situation on more than the basis of medical advice, I spread out all the trinkets we had left: beautiful batik scarves from Glarus, red silk ribbons, and packs of chewing tobacco. All this would be theirs, over and above the arranged pay – already high for Greenland – once everything was carried up. And the Greenlanders' leader, the often-mentioned Vitus, was told in private that he could look forward to a complete linen suit, which I would have delivered to the west coast.

This gave us a businesslike basis on which to begin our activities. The loads were divided up and the march started. We had decided to use the next few days to ferry everything halfway up to the edge of the lakes. We all valiantly tackled the job, even though almost all of us were semi-invalids. Fick was still hurting from his fall into the ship's hold. Mercanton had sprained an ankle on the first march to the ice cap. Hössli had dug an ice-axe into his leg and apparently damaged a tendon. Jost had slipped on one of the climbing slopes with a load of seventy-five pounds on his back, which did nothing for his fitness. What worried us most was Gaule's infection, which looked more and more like blood poisoning and obviously weakened him. In this condition, it was no small thing to lug the heavy loads over trackless rocks, defenceless against persecution by the mosquito swarms. And all the time the broad "Ajorpok, ajornakrak" of the Greenlanders ("It's no good, it does not work anymore") resounded in our ears. There is not one among us who will not remember for years to come every stone from the depot on the shore, the "mosquito hell," the "hole," the "mosquito place," and then up over the rocks to the middle depot.

Those who were bearish in their speculations thought it would take at least two weeks to carry everything up to the ice cap. In the meantime, the sun would get its chance to ruin our sledging route in the rim zone. We needed to know as soon as possible how fast the melting at the ice rim was advancing and how far the western party would have to accompany us on the ice. If we could reduce our escort, we would need to haul much less material up to the ice.

Mercanton, Jost, and I therefore left once more for the ice cap to reconnoitre and also to carry up three more loads. We found that half the snow along the moraine had melted since our first visit. The rivulets of meltwater had started to erode the ice. But, for the time being, things would work reasonably well. We walked about twelve kilometres inland and had the impression that we could do without the sledges of the accompanying western party.

What a view to the east! Waves upon waves of ice and finally the utmost horizon, the one we would have to reach. "What a sight," murmured Jost. "Forever and ever, amen."

On the return trip, we kept more to the right until we could overlook the whole rim of the ice cap from the area at the Eqip Sermia to the Torsukatak and even further to the great Karajak glacier. The peak that stuck up sharply in the distance – wasn't this the Ainuk, the peak I had once climbed with Dr Baebler in order to have a first look at the ice cap? But nothing I had ever seen matched the view we had from here: the ice cap flows down on a front almost one hundred kilometres wide from a higher step about thirty kilometres away, so that the separate glaciers on the coast look like branches of an enormous stream at high water. It was immediately clear why this part of the coast had to be the place of origin of all the masses of icebergs that are discharged into the sea here.

When we returned from our scouting mission to the picturesque disorder of the camp near the "middle lake," we found that, fortunately, the pile of gear had grown considerably. Our companions looked strangely changed, with hands and faces as black as Moors. This was the mosquito ointment that wise old Stolberg had found after a long search and had included as an invaluable part of his kit. The novices had not appreciated this unappealing substance, and had even suggested that we leave it behind. But now! A few hundred mosquito bites had transformed their noble foreheads into surfaces of indescribable lumpiness, and substantially changed the judgment made inside these foreheads on the virtues of the Moorish ointment. Now the once-dismissive were diligently blackening every exposed spot. That would work for a day. The resulting enhancement of our complexions, however, was to last as far as the east coast.

We had believed that the middle camp would be free of mosquitoes, but that now proved to be a big mistake. The best I could do was to describe the rim of the ice cap as the closest thing, within reach, to paradise on earth. And we would get there, baggage and all, according to my calculations, within two or three days.

"How lovely the step of the messenger who announces peace ..." To our astonishment, our sweet song of peace from the mosquitoes found no echo. The bearish party was probably disappointed that their negative forecasts would prove to be so wrong. But they were. After three days, everything was up on the ice cap. When the last item was there, the rains came, which had mercifully spared us during the entire transport phase.

I was pleased that my own birthday party fell at a time when working strenuously in our common cause had really welded the expedition together. We now knew from experience that we could rely on each other. For the celebration, I was led into the tent of the western party. Gaule, who can be quite sarcastic, marched gravely in front like a standard-bearer with what he considered appropriate emblems: an ice pick and a dog whip. Why the dog whip? Mercanton, with his mastery of the French lexicon, managed to express in his delicate way the undeniable fact that I was a hard taskmaster, and to mention that tyranny as a form of government really belonged to antiquity. But Greenland and the ice cap are antiquities! He nevertheless found rhetorical ways to offer, with a good conscience, the two bottles of non-alcoholic wine he had carted up, sweating and toiling, for the tyrant's celebrations.

On the last day of the transport, Hössli and two Greenlanders had brought up the dogs from the seashore, no easy task. The dogs had become quite unruly after being tied up and idle for so long. Unfortunately, one had to be shot on shore because he was badly wounded. The Greenlander who peeled off the skin, which he kept for himself, grinned and said, "Twenty kroner." That had been the price of purchase.

I still had a job of literary work to do down on the shore. I wanted to give to the kayakman who was leaving with our last mail a letter in Greenlandic for the headman of the nearest Eskimo settlement, to let him know what to do with mail and that we would wait another three days at the rim of the ice cap for long-expected mail from the *Hans Egede*.

I might mention that this chore gave me great satisfaction, because I could overcome an old complex. During ten years of schooling, there had been pressure to hand in essays and compositions without mistakes. This had once weighed heavily on my psyche. Today I was free and had the pleasure of writing a document I knew could not provide a margin wide enough for all the red correction marks. What mattered was that the man in Ata understood what I wanted to say!

But, no chance! Jens, the saintly dog herder, turned out to be a notable Eskimo scholar. He read my letter with a smile and proposed that we write a second version together.

In our last mail was a letter to a friend of the expedition, Professor C. Schröter, of the Schweizerische Naturforschende Gesellschaft, where we emphasized again that, if our ice cap crossing turned out badly, it should not be concluded that the preparations had been insufficient. No one should use this as an argument against similarly risky enterprises. By a strange coincidence, this letter would be read at the General Meeting just moments before the news of the expedition's success arrived.

For three days, while we waited in fog, rain, and snow for the kayak messenger to return, we repaired the dog harnesses and packed the three sledges.

It might be of some interest to set out what kind of gear we took for the ice cap. Peary once said that, in an emergency, one could do without a tent on the ice cap. But if there is no emergency, one would really miss it, especially if exact scientific measurements had to be taken on the way. After testing a variety of materials, we had our tent made from Swiss military tent cloth. I picked a dark colour to rest the eyes inside the tent, and also for warmth in the sun and so that it could easily be seen from a distance against the snow. The entrance, of Fick's special devising, was like a tube made from light-coloured material that could be tightly sealed. Opposite, adding to the rectangular floor area of 2 by 2.4 metres, there was a triangular bay that we called the "apse." This way, the tent offered less resistance to wind. At the top of the apse was a window that could be tied closed. The tent poles were made of three-centimetre bamboo, the floor was sewn to the sides, and there was a separate waterproof floor sheet that could double as a sail if necessary. All the parts for the rigging of the sail were tried and tested, and could be put up within minutes. For the western party, we had a tent of strong raw silk, light but not quite windproof.

Our favourite pieces of equipment were the sleeping bags made from the skins of young reindeer. They were relatively light and as warm as you could wish. Wrapped up inside, one felt as snug as in Abraham's lap. These we kept in waterproof bags. Other protections against the cold included one pair of double fur boots for each of us, a pair of fur mittens, and a down-filled jacket. We usually did not need all of this on our march, only when we had to stand around with the instruments or sit quietly in the tent. En route, our thick woollen clothes and underwear and our lightly hobnailed Swiss ski boots, spacious enough for three pairs of thick socks, afforded sufficient protection. Moreover, we had four roomy overalls of Vadaline, a strong, windproof material, for protection against strong gusts and penetrating blowing snow. We looked like clowns in them but were otherwise quite satisfied.

We used ash skis. Fick and Gaule had also wanted to take a pair of so-called Swedish cross-country skis, which are narrower and much longer than ordinary skis and somewhat broader at the tip. They are supposed to run more smoothly on obstacle-free flat terrain.

Besides the sleeping bags, the most highly valued piece of equipment was our stove. We used the kerosene Primus, so popular in the North. The advantage over alcohol is its higher calorific value. The Primus makes good use of its kerosene, which is vaporized and mixed with air, as in a soldering lamp.

On Shackleton's advice, I bought a set of aluminium pots similar to the Nansen cooker, which utilizes heat efficiently. We had thirty litres of kerosene, carried as a precaution in three metal canisters and packed separately in the three sledge boxes. We used only about twelve litres.

On our trek through the icy desert, we guarded the three boxes that, besides the kitchen equipment, contained the instruments and books, almost as carefully as the Children of Israel watched over the Ark of the Covenant on their desert wanderings.

The heaviest part of the load was, of course, the food and the pemmican, packed in blocks of 250 and 500 grams and soldered into large tins weighing 20–25 pounds. (A metric pound is about 500 grams). All in all, we had 820 pounds (420 kilograms) of pemmican, which we considered adequate to feed the dogs for four weeks and ourselves for eight. A daily dog ration was between 330 and 450 grams. We each received at least half a pound a day. Besides pemmican, we had Maggi soups, dried vegetables, Lenzburg jams, canned meat, condensed milk, and a popular powdered milk-coffee, not to mention honey, butter, cheese, and dried sliced apples. Not that these comestibles were freely at our disposal, of course. An iron law, with Hössli as its guardian, assigned each one of us his daily ration, measured to the gram and the millimetre. Only with our cheese was Hössli less pitiless. Making an exception to the rule, he distributed it exponentially, calculated on the portion left over. Only on our arrival at the east coast depot – although I am getting ahead of myself here – did the asymptotic cheese curve, owing to our appetites, suddenly drop to zero.

Among our provisions, I have almost forgotten to mention our black rye bread. I regret that I did not bring home at least one piece as an exhibit, because it was so hard that I believe nobody's teeth, nor in fact any description, could do justice to its solidity. We would diligently chew for five minutes on these blocks, as a burglar would work on a safe, with no real hope of success. Only the endless polar day, I am certain, kept us from seeing the sparks showering from our teeth. It is this hard bread that made us of the eastern party stray from the true path of social virtue in distributing and packing our portion of the foodstuffs. We annexed the whole ration of biscuits without asking for a general consensus, being of the righteous opinion that the western party would have more opportunity to vary their menus than we did. As we shall see, however, our enjoyment of these purloined biscuits was not to last long.

On 19 June, the kayak messenger Vitus returned from Ata without the hoped-for mail. The *Hans Egede* had not arrived. Thus we started our trek across the ice without any news from Europe since our departure. But perhaps that was for the best. There might have been some message that could have sapped the energy of one or the other of us.

CHAPTER 7
TO THE INLAND ICE LAKE

Now we had no more reason to hesitate. Overnight a light fluff of snow had fallen on the hard uneven ice surface and would be quite an advantage for the dogs' paws to start with. And so we decided to get under way. With the help of the Greenlanders, the dogs were divided into three teams. They had become very unmanageable during the waiting period. I had a real scuffle with the large one from Jakobshavn, because he had bitten me while I checked his harness. This could not go unpunished, and as there was nothing I could grab we rolled on the ground together. Afterwards he realized who was boss. But in retrospect, I wonder if I had done the right thing, because henceforth he couldn't see me close by without getting agitated. Although he was a good sledge dog, he was so wayward that only Hössli could handle him. The heart of an Eskimo dog is not just defiant but may be despondent as well. And it takes some experience to understand this and take it into account.

To the first sled we assigned the team from Egedesminde, a close-knit group used to working together. This team also had the best lead dog, respected by all the others. Dividing up the other dogs, we had to consider not only the balance of pulling strength within the team but also the friendships that had sprung up among the dogs. These of course we could not guess offhand, and only the unhappy whimpering back and forth between teams in the first two camps showed us where the special attachments lay. Since this was not a question of human but of dog management, and we could follow common dog sense without fearing to set a precedent, it was easy enough to assent to these simple preferences.

Fog patches were drifting along close to the ground when we started at noon on 20 June. It was very hard to keep the dogs back. They were howling and, in their impatience, ripped their traces, which had been softened by the rain over the past few days. Soon, however, they found it hard going, and we all had to help. To begin with, we moved up a steep incline through the mushy snow that covered the rim area and fortunately bridged the gap in the moraine, right up to the bare ice. The next zone was a slope riddled with innumerable cryoconite holes and small rivulets. When we had reconnoitred earlier, these streams had barely existed. Now they had etched themselves more deeply so that we had to find another route for the sleds. This still did not keep them from tipping over from time to time. But that was not the worst. A much greater concern was that the dogs were hurting their paws on the sharp edges of the cryoconite holes when they broke through. Soon a red trail of blood marked our route. The five Greenlanders hired to accompany us to the first camp looked much more worried than was justified because they were hoping that we would stop early.

We set up our tent at an altitude of 840 metres, and again we all sat together for a little farewell meal. The western party, which would stay on the coast, again expressed their praise for the eastern party, and, for the occasion, those who were to go across found some pleasant words for the western party.

Stolberg gave me some mail and greetings for the family at home, and then he turned west again with three of the Greenlanders. Mercanton, Jost, and the two Greenlanders, Jens and Emil from Jakobshavn, were to remain with us until the next day. That made for a cozy night, eight in a tent made for four, but it worked.

The following day we set our course a little too far to the right and for a while hit an area riddled with crevasses. This was a novelty for the dogs and, although they managed adroitly, one or the other would slip off or break through, kicking and struggling in their harnesses until they were rescued. In the second half of the day, we unexpectedly happened upon one of those wide, swift, and deep streams that enliven the rim area in a way that rather hindered our progress. To cross it would have meant completely unloading the sledges, a wearying, time-consuming work. As we found out in the end, the detour we made to the right did not take any less time. The stream came from a half-frozen lake surrounded by a snowy "marsh" at the bottom of one of those vast flat ice depressions that characterize the surface of the rim area.

While Jost came back from our advance scouting to guide the sleds onto the best track, I went far ahead and realized that a whole chain of lakes barred the way to the right, whereas to the left we would be able to leave the lake region below us by crossing one more water course and climbing a slope. On my return, I found the camp already set up. Men and dogs had had enough after the snowy marshes.

But after my report, we all decided to pack up again and at least cross the unavoidable stream while we still had Jost and Mercanton and the two Greenlanders to help us. The problem was that the latter two did not want to come any further. Earlier, I had given them a little talking-to on the basis of "a man, a word." I reminded them of their promises in Jakobshavn to accompany us for a week. They in turn objected that, after all, they were the only ones to come along after the second day, and that no other man from Jakobshavn had done so. Now our renewed departure made them very distrustful. I had to give them a solemn promise – insofar as far as my broken Greenlandic could sound solemn – that they would soon eat and camp with us, and could then truly go back, right away, with Jost and Mercanton.

A misunderstanding increased the additional march by a good stretch. Hössli, some distance ahead with the first, lighter sled, hadn't realized that the first watercourse he crossed was the real one and had forged ahead several kilometres beyond the spot where we had planned to camp. We had no choice but to follow him with the heavy sleds and the weaker dog teams, pushing, panting, and sweating. However, we were all glad to have put this stretch behind us together. From here on, the four of us would have to do it alone.

Next morning at 9 o'clock, we shook hands once more. Mercanton and Jost had already walked back some distance when Jost returned once again to bring a spare part for the actinometer that had fallen off a sledge on the rough terrain the day before. He would have very much liked to come with us all the way, and though I had my very capable companions, I would really have liked to take him along too. But Mercanton needed him more on the west coast. And there was also their winter program! And so they went down the icy slopes to the west, waving once more. Then only their heads were visible, then their caps, and then they were gone. We lowered the flag and started our scientific chores.

Our second camp was at an altitude of about one thousand metres. There was still no snow cover anywhere, and on the march the dogs trod more gingerly on the hard ice crystals. In the middle of the third day, we finally reached the snow we had been waiting for. However, the ground was often treacherous. Deep under the snow, the meltwater was dammed up on the slightly sloping base and formed a mush with a barely frozen top layer that would only just support a man's step. So these were the "snow marshes" that had halted Nordenskjöld's further progress in this area. The thought of them had secretly worried me. They were the reason I had planned our departure from the west coast as early as possible. Had we waited another two weeks, they would probably have stopped us too. Even now, we broke through into the metre-deep mush and found it safer to put on our skis. There were now hardly any surface streams left, but a mighty groundwater stream supplied round lakes of blue-black open water, which, to our astonishment, filled many of the wide, flat depressions even up here.

On this day we saw the coast once more. Glittering, the waters of Disko Bay shone golden through a gap in the Pakitsok Fjord. That was the last time, until we could shout "Thalatta!" on reaching the east coast.[1]

As the deep snow turned much too soft under the daytime sun, we decided to start the next day's march in the evening. However, we had to wait until after midnight for the snow to be firm enough to carry us.

That evening I had an eerie experience that philistines will find hard to accept. I had some work to finish outside while the others were already asleep in the tent. Suddenly I saw in the white, feathery entwined clouds in the eastern sky a huge, contorted, sneering face. Usually I am the last person to look for fancy cloud pictures. But was this the genie of the ice cap waiting for us? I remembered what I had been told by someone who knew what he was talking about: "To carry out your plan means your certain destruction." But what could go wrong? Our sleds were laden with ample food supplies, our equipment was carefully selected and tested, the dogs were strong, we had reached the snow, the crevasses were behind us!

The answer came the next day. We had been under way for about three hours when, before their leader was aware of it, the foremost team ventured onto the ice of a lake almost covered with snow. The dogs' paws found no footing on the blank, new ice, and the sledge stuck fast.

In no time the rivalrous dogs of the following sleds caught up, but they too could go forward no further. I happened to be beside the last sledge checking the sledge meter. As the situation looked serious, I shouted to Hössli to whip the dogs ahead immediately. But it was too late. While the first team could just reach firmer ice, the ice cover broke under the weight of the others. I got only a glimpse of Fick's sledge disappearing into the water when the ice broke under me and under Gaule's sledge with a loud report. "Our beautiful expedition!" I thought as I subsided.

---

1 The reference is to Xenophon's *Anabasis*, in which a detachment of ten thousand Greek soldiers shout for joy on reaching the sea (*thalatta* is the Attic form of the word) after retreating from a failed expedition against Persia.

There was no firm ground under my feet, but above me, the runners of a sledge and a helping hand gave me a chance to work myself up onto firmer ice. Only a corner of Fick's sledge was visible; it still seemed to be somehow afloat. The front of Gaule's sledge was still on the ice, but it broke through when we tried to push it ahead. The first task was to cut the dogs loose, and if possible, find ropes in one of the sledge bags in order to anchor the sledges to the firm ice to keep them from disappearing altogether. When we tried to approach the accident spot, more and more ice kept breaking away. Again and again, we sank up to our necks in the icy water and had to find our way out on our own.

We finally managed to extricate two pairs of skis from the sledges and put them on despite our frozen fingers. Now we could ever so carefully approach the sledges. Fick, working half-submerged, cut loose one piece of baggage after the other from his sledge, and Gaule pushed them onto firmer ice. Hössli and I did the same thing with the other sledge.

The wearying work went forward with extreme slowness. With hands that had lost all sensation in the water, we hardly knew what we were about as we sliced into our hands instead of the ropes. No chance to warm them in our pockets, as the cold wind had frozen our clothes into icy armour. We hardly knew which was worse – to be out of the water or in it. There would come a moment when we would be too numb to do anything more. But, thank God, the bundle with the sleeping bags flew out onto the solid ice.

For the first time I could breathe a sigh of relief. They would save our lives. Then came the cooking box. A second deep sigh: this meant that the expedition, the crossing, could continue. Finally, we could jerk the greatly lightened sledges out of the water. We had spent three anxious hours salvaging them, and time and again we had broken through, often up to our necks. I was so stiff in my frozen clothes that I could no longer bend and afterwards had to crawl flat on my stomach into the tent.

When we reviewed the casualties from this bath, we found that all the instruments were unharmed, above all the chronometers. The tent and most of the fur clothes were safe. As a precaution, I had put them into waterproof bag, and on the coast, Fick had soldered up the cans containing the ration of matches and distributed them between all the sledges. All these precautions had now paid off.

My own chronograph had unfortunately swallowed some water and refused to function; but my old fondness for precision mechanics and watch-making came to my aid and I managed to get it going again. Our beautiful stereoscope was beyond repair; as Goethe says in *Faust II*, "Wire and glue will not hold together for ever." The wooden case of the theodolite was so badly warped that we could not take the instrument out for several days for fear of damaging it. During that period, we had to interrupt our magnetic observations. A bag of angmagsettes was lost entirely. We had planned to use these fish as dog food to ease the transition from normal fodder to pure pemmican. I'd like to know how future wanderers on the ice cap might explain the discovery of an unexpected population of fish in that lost lake. Taking unkind advantage of our helplessness while we were busy saving our sunken belongings, the dogs made up for the loss of the angmagsettes by chewing up their traces and harnesses. In some cases, when we could not interrupt their fun, they left only the ivory buttons. While three of us tried to thaw and dry themselves out in the tent, the fourth one had to sit with chattering teeth outside and keep an eye on the dogs. This is the moment when we realized the sterling worth of excellence in dog management.

The most serious aspect was not what we had lost in the accident but what we had gained – namely, a hundredweight of unwelcome water, which had soaked our zwieback rusks, bread, and biscuits and turned them into permanent blocks of ice. It took all the ingenuity of our quartermaster, hungry stomachs, and all the goodwill of my companions to find any taste left in them. I felt great satisfaction to see that none of us had been disheartened by our lacustrine episode, which could so easily have been fatal. On the contrary: it had actually encouraged us to know that we had been able to extricate ourselves from a very serious situation, and that the many precautions we had taken in putting our equipment together had proved so successful. The next day we started at the normal hour as if nothing had happened.

First, we had to work out how to get away from the lake – which we later called our "summer-bath" – for we had not really reached dry land as we had assumed. Rather, we were only sitting on the firmer ice cover in the middle of the lake, which was separated from the "shore" partly by thin and treacherous ice, and partly by open water, as we now realized. However, in the evening, Hössli had scouted out a traverse that would become more reliable in the overnight freeze-up.

On this and the following days, I always went one or two kilometres ahead of the others to watch for lakes. The day after our bath, we quite unexpectedly met a sentient being, a seagull that sat on a frozen pool and watched thoughtfully as our caravan moved along. Had a storm carried him into this desert? Was he hungry? I would have loved to let him know about the angmagsettes in the lake, but we couldn't make ourselves understood.

Plate no. 1
Steamer passage to Greenland, 1909.

Plate no. 2
Campsite at Ikerasak: *left to right*,
Alfred de Quervain, August Stolberg, Emil Baebler, 1909.

Plate no. 3
Korok Fjord at Godthaab, while climbing Saddlen, 1909.

Plate no. 4
The view eastwards from the summit of Kingitoarsuk, 1909.

Plate no. 5
Kayaker with white camouflage screen at Vaigat Sound, 1909.

Plate no. 6
Woman repairing a kayak at Godthaab, 1909.

Plate no. 7
Women flensing a seal at Godthaab, 1909.

Plate no. 8
Ice ledge in the harbour at Godthaab, 1909.

Plate no. 9
Inuit children at Nugsuak, 1909.

Plate no. 10
Stranded iceberg at Godhavn, 1909.

Plate no. 11
The *Hans Egede* ice fast at Umanak, 1909 (*above and overleaf*).

Plate no. 12
The church at Umanak, 1909.

Plate no. 13
A hunter with his dogs at Ikerasak, 1909.

Plate no. 14
Reconnoitering the ice cap's crevasse zone, 1909.

Plate no. 15
Emil Baebler and Alfred de Quervain crossing a crevasse, 1909.

Plate no. 16
Edge of the Karajak glacier, 1909.

Plate no. 17
On the Karajak glacier, 1909.

Plate no. 18
Igner Ohlsen, daughter of the expedition's host, at Sarfanguak, 1912.

Plate no. 19
Rocky fjord, probably at Holstensborg, 1912.

Plate no. 20
Kayak laid up on rocks, probably at Disko, 1912.

Plate no. 21
Outing in the kayaks at Holstensborg, 1912.

Plate no. 22
Inspecting a kayak, 1912.

Plate no. 23
The *Thorwaldsen* at Holstensborg, 1912.

Plate no. 24
Angular iceberg, 1912.

Plate no. 25
The *Thorwaldsen* under sail, 1912.

Plate no. 26
The 1912 expedition members: *left to right*,
Jost, Stolberg, de Quervain, Hössli, Mercanton, Fick.

Plate no. 27
Hans Hössli, *second from right*, with two Greenlanders and a Dane, 1912.

Plate no. 28
Children with husky puppies at Sarfanguak, 1912.

Plate no. 29
The expedition ship *Fox* at Holstensborg, 1912.

Plate no. 30
Sledge rigged with sail, Fick and Gaule, 1912.

Plate no. 31
Launching a pilot balloon, Jost on the right, 1912.

CHAPTER 8

OVER THE TOP OF GREENLAND'S FIRN REGION

After our bath in the lake, we entered into a relatively regular routine but not in any normal or conventional sense. We followed the progress of the sun and always made night into day or day into night, as it suited our progress.

There was thus a certain order to our work, whether by day or night, which after a while evolved into a smooth system. This I shall describe, starting with the precious moment of the day when we decided on a campsite. I took the distance readings on arrival, and we patted ourselves on the backs, more or less, depending on the progress made. In the meantime, Hössli and Fick had pitched the tent, lined up exactly according to the wind's direction, and Gaule tied up the dogs to the long sides of the sledges, to keep them still (in case they had other plans). By then I had taken off my snow gaiters and my boots, for in our tent the rule was as strict as in a mosque – one must not enter wearing boots, only kamiks – and slid inside to attach the waterproof floor sheet and take and arrange the equipment handed to me from outside. First came the precious case for the instruments and books, our "ark of the covenant," which went into the tent's apse to weight it down against the wind. Then came sleeping bags and the cooking chest and so on, each being placed in its exact spot, precise to the decimetre and centimetre.

I don't want to tax the patience of outsiders or the credulity of insiders beyond reason by describing in more detail the superb order that reigned in our tent. But I revel in the memory, for never in my whole life have I been even remotely as well organized as I was on the ice cap. What does this prove?

As far as I am concerned, one thing was clear. How much better off, that is to say happier, a man can be without letters and newspapers. Give me any day an average snowstorm in preference to a full letterbox. What are these missives other than a thousandfold curtailment of one's freedom? How marvellous it is to go one's own way for a change, rather than to follow the zigzag route of obligations or to kowtow one's respect like an obsequious mannequin. And so we went on our way, our very own way without signposts or rulings from any authority or other power. It was as Busch says:

> Ohne einen hochgeschätzten tugendhaften Vorgesetzten
> Irrt er in der Welt umher,
> hat kein reines Hemde mehr.

> (Without a highly esteemed / virtuous master, / he wanders through the world / without a clean shirt left.)

Alas, the latter point was all too true. But one takes that in one's stride.

Back to the order of the day. First came the feeding of the dogs. While our cooker droned away, slowly digesting lumps of ice in the pot, we hastily opened a twenty-five-pound tin of pemmican in the tent and chopped the one-pound pieces into smaller portions to make them edible for the dogs and distribute them as fairly as possible. The dogs soon got to know the sound of this process. Just tying them side-on to the heavily laden sleds was not really enough to restrain them properly. Almost nothing can stand in the way of a dog team. Using word and gesture and whip in hand, Fick had to go from team to team to keep them back. To pass the time, the dogs then got at each other's throats. The pitiful howls of the defeated ones could be heard in the tent, interspersed with Fick's calm admonitions for order: "Ei, ei, lexei!" In the meantime we had measured out the portions and leapt out of the tent, each to his own team. Woe on us if we served one team even a couple of seconds after than the other ones. After half a minute, there was nothing left of the twenty-five pounds, not even a speck the size of a pinhead. Yet the dogs were by no means satisfied, as pemmican expands slowly in the stomach, and they went off looking for dessert. It was always Gaule's lead dog, Kutlipilik, "the one with the tear in his eye," who set the bad example. We had taken him from the pastor in Jakobshavn in exchange for one of the yellow curs. His evocative name in no way prevented him from being a greedy fellow, so we had to make an example of him and some of his gluttonous chums by tying their snouts closed.

After feeding the dogs, it was our turn. We, the masters, lived mostly off the crumbs from the dogs' table. We used the small pieces of pemmican we had left and Maggi soup to cook a kind of mush, so thick that a spoon really would stand up in it. On the grounds of some study of pemmican's digestibility, I had been advised against taking it with us. But I held fast to Otto Nordenskjöld's dictum: "I know only that a few bowls of the stuff will keep you going for another day." And so it did.

While the soup was on the stove, I did my own private cooking with the boiling point apparatus, the so-called hypsometer, for our daily aneroid check. This determines the boiling point to 1/300th of a degree Celsius. Without these important measurements, we would not have been able to determine our altitude accurately enough. I managed to get the delicate apparatus safely through all the dangers of our camping life. It is still a matter of contention which of the accidental spills and mishaps in the tent were due to neglect and which an act of God. Opinions were divided, and my companions thought that my own was too rigorous. But it really was too far to go to the nearest department store.

After our evening soup, which on good days was followed by tea or milk to quench our thirst, Gaule put up the instrument to measure atmospheric electricity, someone would fill the cooking pot with snow, ready for the "morning," and someone else took the meteorological measurements. Only then could we sneak into our sleeping bags (Mercanton's expression). There is nothing better than to fall asleep in a reindeer sleeping bag on the ice cap after a hard day's work, except maybe to be wakened by the call "Coffee is ready!" Our enjoyment of breakfast was often interrupted if it happened to coincide with the moment when the sun crossed the first vertical. That was when we had to make our observation for calculating longitude. Usually Gaule observed with the sextant and I watched the chronometer. After breakfast, our quartermaster gave us such goodies out of his horn of plenty as dried apple slices or prunes, to keep by us as snacks for the day. Then we allowed ourselves an hour or so to read or to talk. After that, everyone went to work. Fick measured the snow depth and checked the incline of the slope in various directions with the theodolite. Hössli treated possible patients with scraped noses and swollen lips, wounds that occurred here as on any glacier tour, and which we accepted as a matter of fact. A particularly hard job of his was to deal with the mischief that the dogs never failed to let loose during the night. I kept the scientific diaries up to date and shared with Gaule the task of calculating our astronomical position and the local magnetic variation of the compass. Both were indispensable for determining the direction of the next leg of the march.

We solemnly plotted the longitude and latitude of the camp on the grid of our map, and more or less rejoiced at our progress. How many compass sightings, how many thousand weary footsteps it takes to advance even a small way toward the southeast on the map. However, more and more small steps added up to a systematically advancing line. In order to take the shortest route across the ice cap, like sailors, we could not keep the same compass heading all the time, but had to change direction a fraction more to the right from day to day. At the same time, the magnetic declination diminished considerably, by coincidence in the same measure as the change in our great circle course. In the end, our direction barely changed relative to the magnetic meridian and ran almost parallel to it.

After finishing all the measurements and calculating the day's course, we started to pack up. Half an hour before we were ready to leave, I went ahead on skis to set the direction. The dogs easily followed the track, quite eagerly in the morning and with lagging enthusiasm in the evening. The sledge drivers ran beside the sledges, helped to push when the going was difficult and took a ride when everything went smoothly.

During the first days, the layer of old snow that covered the ice still softened considerably during the daytime. At night, the surface hardened and the sledges ran more easily. But the dogs preferred the soft snow, as long as they did not break in too deeply. On a hard surface, they hesitated to apply all their strength because it hurt their paws.

To our astonishment, we still met deep crevasses every now and then, even when we were already far into the firn region,[1] but we could turn them or cross them on good snow bridges. The situation could get quite unpleasant when the sky became totally overcast and snow started blowing around. Then we could literally no longer see the ground under our feet, and there was always the danger of losing sight of our companions ahead or behind.

During the first three weeks, the wind blew against us almost incessantly, sometimes at storm strength. On clear days the wind direction was quite constant, so that we used it to set our course. The front-runner made a very exact check of the wind direction with his compass roughly every kilometre, and in between he kept the direction with a fluttering red silk ribbon that we had meant to give to Igner Ohlsen in Sarfanguak but which had now found a more practical destiny. When the sun was shining, we took our bearing by checking the sun's position with the compass from time to time.

---

1 The firn region is the intermediate zone between snow and glacial ice.

After a few days I had the idea of calculating a little sundial and drawing it on one of my skis. It marked the direction of the shadow of a ski pole, as it had to fall on the ski every half hour, if the skis were on the right course. The sundial clock proved to be quite practical. Toward the east coast, however, it tended to run fast, like the clocks in the Emmental. No harm done, as long as we were aware of it.

It sometimes happened that the wind fell away altogether, and if fog wrapped the whole area, it was practically impossible to keep the correct direction. Everyone then grumbled secretly or aloud about the front-runner, but none of us who tried it could do any better.

The sorrows and joys of our daily marches are best illustrated by quoting the diary:

27 JUNE, 8 p.m., in the tent, camp 7, 1,450 m altitude

A gale of wind rips off chunks of snow and blows them over the tent. On the day after the lake bath on the 25th, we advanced from 1:30 a.m. till 10 a.m., as if nothing had happened. I put on skis half an hour before the others in order to look out for lakes. After seventeen kilometres, it so happened that we set up tent exactly on Peary's route as the latitude measurements showed. Here about a metre of snow lay on the bare ice. On the 26th, we made only fifteen kilometres between camp 5 and camp 6. We might have gone further, but early in the day the dogs had suffered on the hard ice, and we wanted to spare them. The yellow-red one in Fick's team, the one we call "the swine," hasn't been pulling for a day, and now Ersilik in our team is also on strike. We let them run free. The dogs have started to be permanently hungry and are eating their harnesses. That is Hössli's special concern.

This morning (the 27th) in camp 6, Gaule, who is the breakfast cook, kicked over the freshly brewed breakfast tea. Tragedy! We had to do with what we could scoop up from the tent floor. Today on the trail, strong winds were already against us, and we were still passing more lakes. We made only 14.2 kilometres. Our aim is to advance at least 15 kilometres every day. We believe this is reasonably good for the time being, as we also have to ascend about one hundred metres in altitude every day, with various ups and downs and still almost undiminished loads. In about six days, we might reach the route of Nordenskjöld's Lapps. We'll soon be beyond the Jakobshavn glacier, and yet there are still more crevasses, still more lakes! These are deep blue and ice-covered in the centre. So far the weather has been good, if we do not count the tiresome wind. But to the northwest, it looks threatening.

29 JUNE, 7 a.m., in camp 8, before leaving

The threat came to pass. At the last campsite, the wind grew stronger and turned into a gale that blew all through the night. We postponed our departure since the barometer was rising and we expected the wind to abate, which it actually did. This time I went only fifty to two hundred metres ahead of the dogs. The wind was warm, foehn-like, and the skis did not glide too easily. I was not feeling well and had to push myself hard. Yet we made about twenty kilometres. Last night, we tied the muzzles of all the dogs except Mons's, and we also kept a real dog watch throughout the night. We have grown wiser after all the mayhem.

29 JUNE, camp 9

Today 21.5 kilometres! The character of the "landscape" has changed. We travelled across an endless plain; the horizon is level all around us. Only at kilometre 4 was there an almost totally frozen-over lake (the last one). After kilometre 18, we again saw higher elevations to the left. At this campsite, we are surrounded by a double horizon, proving that we are on a slight hillock. As soon as we are on soft or sticky snow, the distances we estimate by the number of ski pushes and the data from the sledge meter no longer quite tally. Measurements that we made to check the matter agree with the skis, in favour of the longer distance.

30 JUNE, in camp 10

At least twenty kilometres today! In the second half, Hössli took over from me as the front-runner. Our dog technique is working out quite well, now that we systematically tie up their snouts every evening. Mons is the only one left free, an excellent character, really, a super-dog. Today between kilometres 3 and 6, we passed an area of tremendous crevasses up to thirty-five metres wide, most of them covered by snow-bridges, but every now and then a yawning chasm gives us a scare. I am reminded of the area in the interior of the Karajak region that we inspected three years ago. But we are now in the hinterland of the Jakobshavn glacier. The stronger flow of the ice seems to make itself felt even this far into the interior.

1 JULY, camp 11, 8 p.m.

In my sleeping bag. That wasn't a bad performance today. From start to finish, we had gale winds of up to twenty metres a second dead against us, sometimes with snow and blowing ice crystals. At first I was the front-runner, then Hössli, then Fick. In spite of all of this, we managed twenty kilometres. The storm goes on, but now we lie snug in the tent, which is slatting. But it is staying put.

Today the barometer fell mightily. Accordingly, we should have reached two thousand metres altitude. PS: At 10 p.m. I crept out to do the inspection tour around the dogs. All is calm, only the super-dog Mons, "the excellent character," is awake and quietly chewing up his harness. *Et tu Brute*? I reproached him for his wrongdoing, gave him a slap, more symbolic than physical, and tied his muzzle the same as for the others. I do not know what happened in his soul, but the next day he avoided not only me but even Hössli, and from then on he was less approachable.

2 JULY, camp 12

Today the wind did let up, but the weather remained dull. A trace of snow had fallen during the night, and at 11 the snowstorm started again. You couldn't see far. That's the way it went, crescendo all day. The wind veers to south and even southwest. As we can't see anything and the wind shifts so often, we have to watch our direction very carefully. It isn't easy for the man ahead, and it's unpleasant for both parties because of the danger of losing each other. Today, for the first time, all of us did a stint as the front-runner (as we would always do from now on). Gaule almost went astray. Deceived by the unsteady winds, he had lost the direction and went out of our sight. At first I swore to myself about his careless pushing ahead and was determined to express myself accordingly later on, but in the end I was awfully glad to see him again as a dark spot when the blowing wind let up for a moment. Despite all this, we travelled a good distance. The dogs liked walking on the fine snow, which covered up the rough surface.

3 JULY, camp 13, the "Lapps' place"

According to the aneroid, we are now at 2,100 metres altitude. We again advanced twenty-five kilometres. On the whole, the track was flat, yet with clear undulations several kilometres long. Our astronomical observations put us at 68°40'47" north latitude and 45°39'50" west longitude, which means that we are on the route of Nordenskjöld's Lapps. However, judging from the difference in their altitude and ours, we must conclude that the Lapps advanced at best half only as far as they claimed. Tonight it is exceptionally calm. By 9 p.m., the temperature had fallen to –13°C.

6 JULY, morning in camp 15

The last two days went well, although the weather closed in again yesterday. It is obvious that the dogs do not want to move on if the leader is too far away. They need to be able to see him, and they are short-sighted.

6 JULY, evening, in camp 16

The battle with the dogs is over, and we are waiting for our soup. This morning we left in fog, everything grey and unfriendly. Whoever goes ahead has to check the compass constantly. After me, it was Fick's turn. I like to see his tall figure ahead. Because the leader has no way to aim at a fixed point in this kind of weather, we arranged that I would take bearings with the fluid compass from the first sledge and signal with a flag whether to bear left or right. This worked quite well. Only it wasn't easy to look at the compass and the flag at the same time and to watch the dogs, who weren't too willing today. When it was Hössli's turn to lead, the dogs perked up. He is their quartermaster too, and they knew that after Hössli it would be feeding time. They hoped to shorten the time to this, the only moment that counts for them, by catching up with Hössli.

SUNDAY, 7 JULY, midmorning, still in camp 16

In the sleeping bag. Overnight there was wind again and a blizzard started. As we haven't had a rest day since we left the west coast, it is Sunday, and as we have done everything quite well up to now, we'll let the wind blow itself out. We can afford it. We made a hopeless stab at taking a fix on the sun to determine our location, but the sun showed for barely a moment, and all we have to show for our pains are cold fingers. The dogs are already snowed in. It is comfortable in the tent. These sleeping bags are indeed "a quality item," as Pastor F. put it. We catch up with our diaries, mend things, and have learned conversations on Mach, Kant, Hume and Schopenhauer. Our small library finds more customers today, and it shows.

Each member's personal contribution to the library was limited by weight. And this is what the library comprises: a volume of Schopenhauer's shorter essays; a Faust; a New Testament in the original language; a Zarathustra and a small collection that my sister had put together; one play each of Sophocles, Euripides, Molière, Lessing, Goethe and Ibsen – the book of six, as we called it. Among these, judging from the grease spots, Lessing's *Minna von Barnhelm* was the most popular. Schopenhauer, with his rabid style of polemics, amused us greatly, and whoever was reading him at the time could not keep from quoting some of the more vigorous parts, while the grim storm howled a fitting accompaniment. Our library also had a secret section: a two-pound volume of Mach's theoretical physics, which Gaule had smuggled, with my acquiescence, in his instrument box. The additional weight was irresponsible, but we wanted to have something for the long winter evenings in case we were marooned for a year in Angmagssalik. The same idea occurred to our medical man, who talked about reading Greek, but he had unfortunately left the Homer, a gift from Pastor Nielsen, in the depot on the western coast. Maybe Stolberg was reading it to his companions.

We are sure that our forced literary preoccupation was not without permanent influence on the history of literature, particularly in the study of Faust.[2]

To the reader, these perspectives may seem somewhat distant from the ice cap. But we in our tent were not distant from the ice at all! These things amused us, and stimulated our imagination when we were cooped up inside, and everything else could be shut out. What an Eldorado this ice cap would be for a misanthrope. With an ice shield of a few hundred kilometres all around, dear but tedious friends, well-meaning enemies, and friendly pests would just have to leave him in peace!

Then there would only be the dogs. And a fugitive from the world would say, "They are easier company than man." However, the following section of my diary is prefaced with: "Name me the dog, oh muse, the glutton who does so much evil…"[3] (I see you sigh, see you wince and frown, my aesthetic and philological friend. But there was never any time to pay attention to syllabic niceties.)

More remarks about dogs: except for their relentless greed, they have worked out better than I could ever have expected. This is partly to the dogs' credit, and partly due to my companions, who got fully to grips with dog affairs. Our lives depend on them, as Administrator Thron had predicted. But most of all we owe gratitude to the lessons at David Ohlsen's in Sarfanguak. How uncertain we would otherwise feel, in the face of these dogs!

We still have all twenty-nine dogs. For the last few days, Ersilik in our team has been pulling again, as does Fick's Swine, though only feebly. In our team, Jack has a lame hind leg and is walking free. Cognac is a rather lazy chap. Whisky, his brother, who feels a rough tenderness for him, bites him and then licks his wounded leg. The two brothers are usually the last to get up, but once in position to start, Whisky howls the most eagerly to rush forward. Kakortok ("the white one") is an excellent, quiet, and diligent dog, always pulling in the middle of the team. Jason with the yellow head is another good one, but an eternal querulant. Ersilik has improved, although he is still a sorry character. He reminds me of a former schoolmate, whereas when I look at Jack and Kakortok I always unwittingly think of some distant relatives of mine. Silke is a most industrious lady, but of

2 There follows an amused, literate comparison of some Goethe and Busch verse, easy to understand only if one knows German literature (EQS).

3 Parody of the opening stanza of Homer's *Odyssey* (EQS).

course also wants to be treated nicely. Mons pulls best of all and so convincingly and dutifully that he hasn't the time to carry his tail high, even when the going is easy. His only bad habit – this may have some dog symbolism – is to keep changing places with Mrs Silke until their thongs are hopelessly intertwined.

Among Fick's dogs, there is timid Parpu, the lead dog with shaggy black fur and glowing eyes, and the little black one who pulls gallantly but is always so sad. Fick's dogs manage better than all the others to weave a Gordian knot with their traces, so that their master has to patiently disentangle them about ten times a day.

In Gaule's team, the preacher's dog, the red Kutlipiluk, and the nasty white one are fighting for dominance. Only Hössli can handle the latter one.

Our dogs sleep tied up to the sledge, the females on top of it. Neither we nor the rest of the dogs dispute this spot. The dogs really treat their ladies with courtesy and respect.

The lady in our team, Silke, is especially trusting. At each stop, she lies down near the sled, beside the seat of the driver, and every time I have to separate the traces, she comes and slides her nose into my hand.

Right now, the whole pack of dogs and the sleds are snowed in, and they betray their presence only by the occasional whine.

9 JULY, morning, before leaving camp 17

Yesterday in the morning, we had a big job digging out dogs and sleds. The snow was so hard-packed by the wind that we had to hack out every piece with our ice-axes. Unfortunately, we found Swine dead. Poor fellow. Then we discovered another unfortunate fact. Most of the harnesses had disappeared without a trace. Hössli, our master harness-maker, had his work cut out for him, and he worked with Eskimo-like skill. But his worried eyes seemed to foresee the moment when we would have to cut up even our shirts for dog harnesses.

We continued our march in good weather, although the winds were still quite stiff, blowing no longer from the southeast but from the east. We left the dogs hungry, and they didn't pull any less for it.

I feel quite relieved that the weather is good. After all, it might have continued to be as bad as over the last few days. Or we might even have had a total foehn! (I could imagine a weather scenario where the wind blew continuously from east to west over the whole ice cap. In that case, we would have met progressively deteriorating weather as we advanced.)

We are now in the geometrical centre of our trek. To celebrate, we splurged on a can of ox tongue yesterday.

10 JULY, at camp 18, in the morning

I am waiting for the hypsometer to boil. Gaule is calculating the astronomical longitude. Fick is outside observing the slope angle. Hössli is mending kamiks. Yesterday we had a good day. Although we overslept by two hours, we still managed thirty-one kilometres. At noon, we made a stop to take the altitude of the noontime sun. This was also the moment when we had to shoot and slaughter our good Jack, whose leg wouldn't heal and who now was only eating the other dogs' food rations. Tonight and tomorrow, we shall have to find out how we and the dogs hold with this meat. We might have to depend on it in an emergency. I started to compare the temperature of the snow at different depths with the air temperature. It is interesting to see how the air temperature moves in line with that of the snow. The day after tomorrow I expect that we will reach the highest altitude of our route over the ice cap.

11 JULY, at camp 19, midmorning before leaving

Hardly slept all night; made measurements regularly to determine temperature curve overnight. It sinks to –20°C. Inside the tent it is almost as cold. When we cook our soup, such a fog forms that we can no longer see each other during the meal. As if in a séance, the ghostlike hand of the quartermaster appears out of a cloud holding a plate full of soup in the direction where he deems me to be sitting. Yesterday was a superb day: thirty-two kilometres in full sunshine, afternoon almost no wind. Now we can sit very comfortably on the sledges. Trap, trap, trap, go the dogs, all by themselves. And the light snow drifts past beside the sledge runners. One sits and dreams a bit and we aren't aware that the temperature has risen to only –7°C, even at noon. Two gulls and a larger bird – a bird of prey? – fly eastward and suggest the hoped-for coast. The fact that the terrain is still rising makes this most remarkable.

Tonight we all ate dog meat, stewed, a bit tough but acceptable. But we were rather sad to think of Jack. On the whole, the slaughtering is very repugnant to us. Even Hössli dislikes it and his unwilling assistant Fick even more so. The dogs first went for the pemmican and then gulped down the meat, but left the heart and liver aside.

12 JULY, at camp 20, morning

These are supposed to be the "dog days," yet our temperature fell to –23°C at night. So far, we have advanced 410 kilometres on the ice cap. It still slopes upward, but less so than in the early days. The theodolite indicates three minutes. On the other hand, there has been a hint of northwest to north winds. What a turn! Today would really be the day to make ski excursions both to the northeast and southwest as far as possible. But yesterday a very suspicious looking fogbank started creeping over the southwestern horizon, and overnight the sky clouded up. The wind is shifting from northeast to east-southeast again and keeps increasing in strength; snow has started blowing around. It is going to be an uncomfortable march, not like the day before when we could still go around in our shirt-sleeves at –10°C.

This morning, Hössli had his first surgical job (besides the now-recurrent slaughter of dogs). Each of us has caught some sort of infection from handling the dogs, which has to be lanced. Gaule, who has not been able to use one of his hands for several days, had to have the deepest incision, and Hössli gave the comforting warning, "Watch it, it's going to itch a bit." Watching made me almost sick, but Gaule kept as still as Mucius Scaevola.[4]

We wait awhile to see if the wind will abate a little. "Er macht's dänk wie dä uf em Dach," Hössli remarked with resignation. Big suspense. What is that man on the roof doing? "Er het's g'macht wie-ner het welle!" was the answer. He's done as he jolly well pleased. From then on "dä uf em Dach" was a well-worn phrase on the expedition, a constant companion on bad days and good ones, almost a fifth member of the expedition, who really had to be introduced too.

13 JULY, at camp 21, morning

Oh yes, yesterday the weather acted "wie dä uf em Dach" with harsh winds from ahead and blowing snow. But we too did as we pleased, grinding out more than twenty kilometres, which would be more than thirty-five kilometres in good weather. We just did it. There are people I know who challenged my predicted average daily distances – and they would have remained in their tents today!

This was quite a production. The front-runner can't see much more than the black tips of his skis ahead of him and, looking back, the three sledges as indistinct black shapes fading into the snowstorm. Although they keep close together, most of the time only the drivers' heads are visible and sometimes everything disappears that is further away than twenty to forty metres. All of us have long icicles on our chins. Yesterday I was only able to loosen my hood after half an hour in the tent. Beard, chin and hood were frozen into single block of ice. Yesterday we tried for the first time to feed the dogs a new way, still in their marching array. The other method no longer worked. Yesterday, they almost overran us and the tent. We let them run loose last night, but took the

---

4 The Roman hero who held his hand over a fire (EQS).

harnesses into the tent. This worked fine, except that they kept making little excursions to the tent, whereupon the man on that side would mutter "Sauhund!" and move away from the wall.

This morning the weather is clearing a little. As the barometer had moved up more than was plausible during the last day's march, we are eager to see Fick's observation of the horizon. He calls into the tent, "It's lower, by eight minutes." I have to go outside. Later: it's really true. We have reached the top of the gigantic dome.

For this occasion, for the first time since Mercanton and Jost left us, I unpack the silken flags of Switzerland and Bern and hoist them on the long snow probe. We name the camp Abwärts (downwards). The high point of the ice cap is actually located so far to the east that we have reached it only after travelling two-thirds of the way. This we had not expected!

15 JULY, at camp 23, morning

There are two days of travel behind us. When I first went ahead after the Abwärts camp, I suddenly felt strangely emotional. By the way, we were descending only theoretically. It didn't feel downhill at all. Quite the contrary. The snow didn't support even the dogs; there was no more "trap, trap, trap." We could not ride along but had to help in the snowdrifts. Again and again, I had to think of Koch and Wegener's plans for the coming year. With horses, the going would be even worse in this powdery snow. On the morning of the second day, we had to dig out the sleds again. There had been a strong wind from the northwest. We put on our wind-clothing, tied the two rear sleds together side by side and put up the sail. I was cursing. (This is specifically mentioned in the diary. It couldn't have been the only time. World history will never decide whether I was right in certain instances, it is really not important. At any rate, my companions were patient men.)

We harnessed the two dog teams one behind the other. This looked rather questionable, but it worked. The wind was a great help, though unfortunately it was less strong than during the night. Today the weather is good, and we are hoping for a fair trip.

16 JULY, at camp 24, morning

Though we left in good weather yesterday, we ended up in fog and snow. Today my dogs simply ran over me while I was loosening their traces. They mistook a signal from the following sledge for their own. I was annoyed, although that didn't help me at all! We have to watch that the teams do not follow each other too closely when we are under way; otherwise we will have a dreadful fight breaking out, one that only a firework display from the whips can subdue. It is often an all but impossible task to let the first team go ahead and try to hold the other ones back a little while, in order to keep the necessary distance. The dogs start howling in one voice full of indignation and tug impatiently at the harnesses.

Last night, we fed one dog to the others. Overnight came a thaw. After trying a while to make progress during the day, we set up the tent again and waited for nightfall, when the surface would freeze, before continuing.

17 JULY, at camp 25, afternoon

Yesterday by midnight we had marched thirty-five kilometres. The sky cleared, the midnight sun appeared so that we could see ahead of us, and it was easier to keep our direction. We now have 526 kilometres of ice cap behind us and we are starting to look out for land, just as a sailor searches for the coast. It may seem curious to note that the dreadful monotony of this most absolute and unforgiving desert never struck us as depressing. The reason may be that, on the one hand, we are sure of our work, and on the other, we have other concerns and know that each day brings its own problems. Of course, if we had to advance in this boundless solitude while uncertain of our objective and direction – the mere thought makes me shudder.

Inherent in this barren waste, there is also a certain grandeur that is hard to describe. It has to be experienced. The sun went to rest for an hour. At dusk, the sky blends with the horizon. Even the three sleds behind me, visible a moment ago as black dots, have disappeared behind a slight rise. Now there is nothing for the eye to focus on. The external world is a complete tabula rasa, where I have the impression that I am the only object and where I am completely on my own to create thoughts and ideas. And this capacity to think alone confirms that I am still a son of this world – until I hear the hot breath of the dogs, who have quietly caught up with me.

CHAPTER 9
EASTERN MOUNTAINS AHEAD!

CAMP 26, 18 JULY, 7 p.m.

Last night, after driving for three-quarters of an hour, at 8:45 p.m. there was yelling and waving from the sleds behind us. Fick with his hawk's eyes had seen land! To the left of our track, far off on the horizon, there was a high mountain and also some lesser ones. They were all much more to the left than I had expected. Today we realized that they had to be an unknown mountain range that is not marked on the maps. We all started to feel pretty good, and we had a perfect run in every respect. The dogs ran as fast as they could. Behind us, there was the crimson sun in the night sky. What a setting! How vast, how broad this solitude is! We shall never forget it. We made an advance of forty-two kilometres. As agreed, we celebrated Fick's birthday on the day we first sighted land. Today I made an exact drawing of the mountainous horizon. It is roughly one hundred kilometres away, at right angles to our course.

CAMP 27, 19 JULY, afternoon

Last night, we travelled forty-five kilometres, most of the time at a canter, sometimes at a gallop. To the left a magnificent mountain landscape has come into sight, consisting partly of the mountains hinted at on the map, probably on the other side of the Sermilik Fjord. Then everything disappeared again behind the icy horizon for a long while, but the first mountain, the dominant one, always remained visible. I named it Mount Forel. Unfortunately, the weather has started to go downhill. At this campsite it is raining. I had great difficulties getting a second exact fix on Mount Forel. Schröter's Nunatak and Meister's Gate farther to the east had already disappeared in the fog. Hössli and I do not feel well. Yesterday, while I was driving the dogs, I threw up, and again today. The dogs do not look too good either. Jason, Whisky, and Cognac do not even want to eat pemmican, and for several days, the dog meat disagreed with them too. They can't digest it at all, and they have bleeding diarrhoea.

CAMP 28, FJORDBLICK (FJORD VIEW), 20 JULY, evening

What a splendid day. Yesterday we were still at 1,500 metres altitude when we started off. Although we knew by our calculations that the fjord had to be close by, the ice surface didn't seem to drop accordingly. Like the Greenlanders when they are amazed, we kept saying "Tupinakrak" over and over again.

At 1:30 a.m., some mountain peaks rose into view over the ice surface, straight in line with our course. They must be part of the mountains on the island of Angmagssalik, far beyond the fjord. At 2 a.m., we sighted some round knolls much closer by, with steep rock faces that dropped off to the left, possibly toward the fjord. I don't like them at all. Something is wrong.

Are we where we think we are? The mountain walls over to the left must be rising beyond the huge Sermilik Fjord, which is still hidden from our view, down there in the depths. But how continuous this wall is! Where is the arm of the fjord that is supposed to cut these off mountains from the island of Angmagssalik? Where is the low-lying area marked on the map that was our goal? And the ice cap does not want to fall off; we are still at 1,300 metres. Are we walking out onto one of those ice-covered knolls similar to the ones we see to our right, and are we going to look down onto the fjord from a rock wall a thousand metres high between two glaciers? Did we arrive too far back in the fjord? By our calculation of the astronomical longitude, this might be possible after all. After being shaken around for four weeks, even the best chronometer could be out that much. But what about the astronomical latitude? This would have to be wrong as well. Yet such an error is inconceivable in the light of our very exact instruments and calculations. But then there was Holm's warning: "Do not trust the map." How far would this hold true?

At 4 p.m., we started to go downhill quickly. We had to improvise brakes with our ice-axes. In theory, this would have been the moment to use David Ohlsen's *imatsiak* method. Suddenly the view onto the fjord opened up. Yes, surely this had to be it, this mirror surface with small chips of ice on it. In reality, these must have been huge icebergs. Still so far away?

We need to think out everything thoroughly before going any further. We set up the tent.

Today the riddles were solved. Kruse's map proved invaluable, since it contained some topographical details on the coast of Angmagssalik that I could finally identify. We can now at least guess the position of the Ikerasak Fjord, even if we can't see it. I made a rough determination of the position of the camp by measuring the angle to those points on the fjord that we had been able to recognize. Gaule does the latitude. They tally.

CAMP 29, 21 JULY at the edge of the ice cap

We arrived at 2 a.m.

Two hours earlier, I had lived through my worst moment on the ice cap. Toward the end, we had hit an area of crevasses after all. I skied ahead to scout out a route. Down here, dusk is already quite advanced at midnight. Without being aware of it, I had gone ahead some distance on the slope, the skis leaving hardly a trace on the hard-packed firn snow. Soon I realized that the slope was too steep, the crevasses too numerous and too open, with unreliable snow bridges. The sledges couldn't get through here. I wanted to wave to the others and signal them to detour. But when I turned around, there were no sledges behind me. Surely they would be hidden behind that nearest ridge. I skied back to a point where I could see as far as the last stopping place. Nothing! Certainly there were some dark spots here and there, but they were the darkness of crevasses in the icefall that dropped from the ice cap to the twilight of the fjord. I stormed back, but my own tracks had vanished, and the crevasses at my side were more numerous than before, and they yawned hungrily. How easy it would be for them to swallow up a miserable sledge caravan! Was it possible, all three sledges? But I knew how eagerly the dog teams sometimes chased each other, almost impossible to hold back. And the incline was so steep! Whether I was searching for half an hour or an hour, I do not know. Finally, up on the slope, I found sledge tracks. What a relief! But it took another hour until I saw my companions and caught up with them. They had stopped following me much earlier and had tried to detour by themselves, convinced that I would see them. I didn't ask for details. For this day, I was finished.

When we reached the rocks of the lateral moraine, we shook hands, not without emotion. We had reason to do so. We had really held together as a team. We hadn't always seen eye to eye on what would be good or satisfactory in this case or that, and I had often had my own way, setting out my objections rather bluntly. But my companions appreciated that I had acted out of my great responsibility and with nothing else in mind than to secure our common success. And they toed the line. An outsider may wonder why I should mention what seems to be self-evident. But anyone who has known similar situations will acknowledge that this is no trifling matter.

So, now we were at the coast. I reverently touched the nearest rock: finally something that was not ice. Hössli, however, the matter-of-fact doctor, had waited for this moment to win the prize, notwithstanding the solemn moment. We had a long-standing agreement that the first man who shouted "Ajungilak!" upon reaching the east side of the inland ice would get Stolberg's farewell cigar, which I had guarded from the first camp onwards. It was clear that he was also susceptible to gentler sentiments when he suggested that we celebrate by letting the dogs run free. The result was an attack on anything and everything edible.

We quickly climbed the wall of the moraine and stacked up huge boulders until we had an unobstructed view to the southeast toward the fjord. This view, however, did not correspond at all with what we expected. According to our map, we should have seen at our feet a smooth shoreline and in the middle of the fjord, not far off, the island of Kekertatsuatsiak. Closer by should be the smaller island of Umitujarajuit. And opposite Umitujarajuit, on our shore, would be our depot.

In reality, there was nothing of the kind. In front of us were three massive rocky ridges extending like three fingers between fifteen and twenty kilometres southward, flanked on the outside by fjords full of icebergs. There were long bays dotted with small islands that seemed to separate the ridges. This landscape made no sense at all.

We had planned to catch up on sleep on reaching the rim of the ice. But the urgency of getting a clear picture of where we were woke us up before time. Gaule and I tried for hours with sextant, telescope, maps, and compass to sort out this puzzling area. Finally, we concluded that we really were at the right spot, according to our astronomical position, but that the map was totally wrong. We knew that it really might not be accurate, remembering what Holm had told me about how this coastal area had been mapped. We doubted that we would be able to find the depot under these circumstances, and in this case, we would try and build a boat from our own materials. In order not to lose any time, we had to divide our forces. And I would make the following agreement with the remaining group, as we always did in such circumstances, in writing and in duplicate:

21 JULY, CAMP 29. Quervain accompanied by Gaule to depart for two to three, possibly four to five days, for the southeast peninsula ("Gauleberg") to explore the region and to find the depot. This I assume to be on the shore on the fjord side of the Gauleberg Peninsula at a distance of about eighteen kilometres. At every stopping point, we shall leave a message about the direction taken. Hössli and Fick will remain in camp 29; will make detailed plans for a boat out of available material; slaughter a number of dogs, and bury the meat securely;

make measurements of the horizon and meteorological observations and look after the chronometers. If we stay away for more than six days, they are to make a check in the direction indicated; then do everything to reach Angmagssalik themselves and to salvage the diaries and records; leave message and emergency rations at camp 29. Departure point for boat journey will in any case be in supposed area of depot.

It was only four days later that I was able to jot down our further experiences in my diary:

On 22 July, at 3:30 a.m., Gaule and I left the ice cap under clearing skies with rather modest rations for three days (mostly pemmican) and emergency rations for two more. We skied southeast along the first ridge (the "Gauleberg"), starting with a long descent on hard snow until our ankles hurt; then we went steeply up through the rocks. There the first plants greeted us, a sad little *carex* that looked miraculous to us, and later a small carnation and a dwarf willow. Now we had a long walk on the ridge ahead. We found it hard to judge distances. The best we could do was to use the various colour gradations as a guide. The rocks close by looked brown, the ones further off were reddish, and the most distant ones purple.

Only toward evening, after a lot of snow-plodding (we had left the skis in the rocks) did we arrive at the end of the peninsula and ascertain the goal of today's trek – that there really is a very large island to the south, namely Kekertatsuatsiak. Thus, our interpretation was right, and here the map was correct.

But where is Umitujarajuit? Would it be, as we first assumed, the red "Celebes" in the maze of smaller islands, or the one out there behind the farthest ridge near the fjord (the "Hössliberg") that had slowly come into view on our walk along the crest? Taking all possibilities into account, we concluded that the latter looked more and more probable. But then we couldn't expect the depot to be down here on the shore, and we would to cross over there. But how? Oh no, more detours!

While we were up on the mountain, we had also used our field glasses constantly to investigate our other problem – namely, to find a route down from our camp near the ice cap. Finally, we found a bay, or rather an ice-free side arm, off the large fjord that led north for twenty kilometres between the Gauleberg and the Fickberg. If we could find the kayaks or if we had to build a boat, here we had a ready-made waterway. What luck – first, that it existed, and then, that we had discovered it!

By the time we had climbed down to the shore from the end of our mountain ridge, it was late at night. We found rather large patches of *Empetrum nigrum*.

With this resinous heather, we kept a signal fire going halfway up the rock face until midnight, enjoying the warmth. Wrapped in our wind clothing, we slept for three hours and then started to build up the fire again. We had taken no cooking pot with us, but Gaule managed to concoct a warm pemmican mush in our one metal cup, which tasted more acceptable than raw pemmican. We left a message that we wanted to scout out the shore of the Gauleberg Peninsula to the head of the bay to the north and then would try to find our way to the fjord.

So we patiently followed the intricacies of the shoreline. But there was no depot. Sometimes we believed, full of hope, that we saw a red flag in the distance. But every time there was nothing there but a red gneiss boulder. Where the rocky shore dipped steeply into the fjord, we often had to ask ourselves if we could get any further. From a distance, we started to worry about one particular spot where a deep gorge reached the sea, the vertical walls cutting the shore apart. How to continue? Could we trust the rotten ice that was still left, long overdue, as it were, adhering to the bottom of the rock face? This was a real trap, especially as it would be easy enough to jump down onto the ice shelf, but surely not to get off it again. Luckily, Gaule discovered a cleft in the rock face that finally gave us a means of climbing around the obstacle. Later came steep smooth slabs that sloped toward the water. Further on, when their angle was less off-putting for a stretch, we could walk for a while and discuss a more philosophical topic, namely the concept and extent of awareness of the present as seen (a) by a child, (b) by the Greeks, (c) by a perfect being. The latter part of the discussion was rudely interrupted by some more appallingly smooth and sloping slabs, which seemed to be only too eager to shed us into the fjord. Our thoughts switched from the general philosophical awareness of the present to the immediate practical present. Later, we walked across a gentle hillside where lush greenery and gurgling streams presented inviting nooks between the red blocks of gneiss, and huge portentous figures seemed to be sculptured in the layers of the rock face: an Our Lady with child, surrounded by wispy pre-Raphaelite angels and solemn Byzantine apostles. We would have willingly surrendered ourselves to the charms of this fairy-tale landscape, but night was falling. Now we were relieved to see the end of the bay ahead.

Then suddenly, as by magic, the scenery changed. A foehn storm broke and chased whitecaps over the water, which just a moment ago had lain still as a mirror. We were glad to have the smooth slabs behind us. The air temperature was 18°C, but the meltwater of the many wide streams at the end of the bay through which we had to wade still felt none too warm.

It was obvious that this foehn blew fairly often from the north. The grass had found shelter in the lee of stones, as on the west coast, and grew there in rows several metres long, aligned with the wind, as if sown by machine. After a short rest, we climbed up the Fickberg's steep escarpment on the other side of the bay. The storm picked up the water from the streams of melt water and flung it in our faces. The wind hurled us against the boulders and, at times, we could move only on our hands and knees. By midnight, it was a little too dim to get a sufficiently clear view of the surroundings. We lay down to sleep behind a big rock, the loaded Browning at our side, for we were already in polar bear territory.

At 5 o'clock, we started our third strenuous day. We aimed southeast, across the Fickberg to the south end of the Hössliberg, first uphill and then across a plateau of horrible black rocks. We kept a sharp lookout to the other side, wondering how far the sea in the valley and the long lakes would get in our way. Nothing spared us: we constantly had to go down to the sea, skirting bays, and then go back uphill again. I should also mention a more light-hearted moment, when we lit up a few dry twigs of dwarf willow to make ourselves a cup of cocoa from our last piece of carefully saved chocolate. On the whole, we could live here, we thought, if only we had more food. But later at noon, on the east shore of the Hössliberg, when the mosquitoes arrived by the thousands, as vicious as they had ever been on the west coast, we definitely saw the advantage of the ice cap and its storms. As we were attacked by the fiendish beasts, I suddenly remembered a little song from kindergarten: "Do you know how many little gnats are a-playing …" And I wished, full of malice, that the versifier was here, who would now be less enthusiastic that "God has counted them all, so that not one will go missing from their whole great number."

By 4 p.m., we were in a position to get an overview of the Hössliberg's southern end. What a depressing vista! Such a jagged coastline, so many bays. What if we have to search everywhere around here!

But there to the east an island came into view, definitely separated from the Hössliberg. This couldn't be anything but Umitujarajuit. It was not long afterwards that I discovered in that direction a pointed object on a rock. A wild hope! I applied my eyes to the field glasses, and there was a stone cairn, large, beautiful, unmistakable! Hot and cold shivers ran through me. We broke into a run. It couldn't be the depot itself, for we were still high on a steep slope, two hundred metres above the fjord. Would there be a message inside? Nothing. But we did find a willow twig stuck into the side, mutely pointing to the northeast. We had been living in the open for so long that we understood this language. Gaule took some steps to the edge of the rocky slope and scoured the area with his glasses in the indicated direction. Sure enough, down there near the shore, there was a second cairn.

We decided to have a banquet with our leftover rations, which amounted to five teaspoons of condensed milk and one and a half thimblefuls of breadcrumbs each. We could afford this luxury. We did our best to make a smoky fire with willow twigs pulled out of rock fissures, in the hope that any Eskimos who might have their summer tents across the fjord would see us. The fjord lay there before us in its enormous breadth, strewn with icebergs.

With care and haste, we climbed down the rock face and reached the area of the second cairn within an hour. Over a rocky hump, we saw a pole sticking out with something red attached to it; the Danish flag. Soon we stood beside the depot. Attached to one of the boxes there was a slip of paper with a laconic message in Petersen's handwriting: "Welcome! The kayaks are down near the shore and the kamiks are inside." Another "velkommen" with the names of all those who had helped to put up the depot was attached to the flagpole. They had also built additional large stone cairns far to the north along the shore of the fjord, all pointing to the depot. What a warm welcome these careful arrangements spelled out, and how grateful we felt!

We set up the large tent we found in the depot and cooked up all sorts of treats, but I didn't feel like eating. Nor could I sleep too well in the tent any longer. Here I have to interrupt my writing and push my hands into the snow for a while. They hurt so much from all the mosquito bites.

Later: we made a large smoky fire up on the bank earlier today. In the afternoon, we tried out the kayaks. If there are Eskimos over there, why isn't anybody coming over?

At 11 at night, we climbed the slope again to make signal fires, letting them burn unattended, which was more practical than carefully supervised regulation fires.

July 26: Enough of these fires. If they haven't seen that, then we'll have to do without them. But what about the dogs?

Early this morning I wrote a note to Petersen including an improved map and also a short text in Greenlandic with a second map and all the Greenlandic designations. We'll leave these messages here in the depot in case someone comes by while we are on our way back to the ice cap. For we have to go now, or the two others left behind will start to worry. We plan to go by water on the route we had discovered, taking all four kayaks. We shall take two kayaks to fashion one large kayak for the two of us, and tow the other two.

By two o'clock in the afternoon, we got away. At first, we had to weave for two hours between icebergs, which were often very closely packed. This felt ticklish. To make matters worse, a southerly wind blew up against us, which grew even stronger when we reached the ice-free side arm, where it blew waves right over our kayaks. The two empty kayaks in tow were dragged so much to the side that we were forever veering off course and drifting dangerously close to the rock face of the "Red Nose." By evening, we had reached the point where the long bay between the Gauleberg and the Fickberg narrows to a width of about fifty metres. There we encountered an ebbing tide so powerful that we gained not an inch in half an hour despite our desperate paddling. Finally, we managed to land on a small rocky island that we called New Sarfanguak, in honour of David Ohlsen's home, and waited for the tide to turn.

We were lucky to find some water so that we could cook some food. We then continued paddling throughout the night, all along the "Bay of Hope," where we had marched so laboriously just a few days ago. At the head of the bay, we beached the kayaks, covered them with stones and started the long and steep route through the rocks and endless snowy slopes to the ice cap, where we arrived around 9 a.m.

The signal flag was there, but it stood lopsided and half-shredded by the storm. The tent? It was gone. Only two sleds were left. Blood was splattered in the snow all around. Here lay a dead dog, and another one stood guard over him and bared his teeth at us. What a sad homecoming! A message in one of the sledge boxes told us that our comrades had moved the tent to the south of the great moraine to find shelter from the wind. And there we found them, and gave them the happy news. We had found the depot and a good route to the sea, and the kayaks were waiting at the beach.

They were glad to see us again. They hadn't had an easy time up there. As Hössli tells it:

> It has been five days since de Quervain and Gaule left and our "far niente" isn't half as "dolce" as one might expect, scarcely as we had imagined after the strenuous crossing of the ice cap. One always feels uncomfortable if an expedition has to split up. All the doubts and uncertainties seem to grow twice as large. In order to fill the long day, we make the usual meteorological observations. Fick, whose steady calmness and composure I have come to know and appreciate very much now that we are alone, has worked out a plan for a real emergency. We would construct a boat from pieces of the tent, the sail, the sledges and the wood from the skis, big enough to take the two of us and the records of the expedition to Angmagssalik. Again and again, we go over the plan, and never in my life have I shown as much interest in boat construction as during these days. We set up the tent where it is sheltered by the moraine, and it is a joy to feel

> solid ground – a large, beautifully veined granite slab – under our soles. We sit for hours on huge boulders the ice cap has deposited here, while our untiring companion is the wild howling of the foehn wind, plunging past on its way from the ice to the deep fjord. In the far distance, several hours away, is the blue Sermilik Fjord with its innumerable icebergs like proud sails moving toward the sea. And to the north a mighty mountain chain, which reminds me of the Alps, lifts itself out of the dark waters. Nobody has ever seen it, no foot has trodden it, and, oblivious to the world, it looks even more solemn and lofty. How marvellous it would be to look out from those peaks onto distant new mountain ranges and the lands stretching away far to the north! But then we turn our eyes back to the southeast, where the open sea, enveloped in a haze, is girdled by a silvery band of dwindling drift-ice, and then our thoughts go far beyond, home to our families, to the green friendly summer of our homeland.

Soon the pale twilight of the short night falls. For the first time, we see the moon rise in the bluish light, giving the landscape an eerie appearance.

And, interrupting this contemplative time, there is the ugly task of killing our good dogs. We cannot afford to use all our provisions to feed them. The animals have done their duty, and their sentence has been pronounced by the Danish administration. Besides, they have now become particularly insolent and aggressive. Yesterday they made a real attack on the provisions sledge and gulped down anything that could be ripped off or was even halfway edible. They are like mercenaries or the "ancient Swiss," impetuous and tough at work and in the struggle against the forces of nature, but they are also intractable ruffians when they have nothing to do.

We prefer to withhold from our readers and ourselves the details of these vile hours, which were for Fick and myself the most difficult ones on the whole expedition. These animals surely knew well enough that their hour had come, yet one followed the other without a sound. I felt I was losing dear and faithful friends, mute companions from another world, where we had worked and fought together.

Tonight we sat longer than usual on the moraine and peered across the land, but there was no movement. Tomorrow they must come back, or the two of us will move on as agreed. This is a disagreeable prospect. What else could await us!

By midnight we are lying in our sleeping bags, in a rather gloomy mood. But early in the morning, our companions wake us up and there is one piece of good news after another. Today we'll have a special menu with all the finest ingredients.

Well, we didn't need to dig up the meat of the slaughtered dogs, or use the boat plan that Fick had so carefully worked out. We were almost regretful! On the 28th at noon, we set out, still accompanied by a dozen dogs that we hoped to save and put on an uninhabited island or take home on the ship. Among them was the little black one from Fick's team. But he refused to leave his dead friend. Side by side, they had come across the ice. Now he remained at his side. No food, no call could change his mind. He never followed in our tracks.

Fick and Hössli duly acknowledged how skilfully Gaule and I had figured out the route down to the Bay of Hope. At this point, we were certainly qualified to write quite a reliable "Guide across the Ice Cap and Surrounding Areas." Our most brilliant discovery during the descent was an enormous three-hundred-metres-high snowbank, which opened a route for our sledges through the rocky cliffs to the valley. Of course, we had to hold the sledges back with our crampons and all sorts of other braking devices to keep them from reaching the valley floor all too suddenly, for there were still some quite deep crevasses to pass.

On the shore of the Bay of Hope, we fed the dogs we were leaving behind one more big meal. Next, we made a depot of everything that would not fit onto the kayak raft, which we loaded up until the hulls were barely above water. We left on the 29th at 6 p.m. It was essential to time our departure properly in order to catch the outgoing tide when passing New Sarfanguak.

For the time being, we were inseparably tied to our vessel, and the diving ducks and gulls that followed us must have seen a peculiar sight. I admit that the adventure of our passage left nothing to be desired. First, everything went smoothly, except that we could not count on Hössli to paddle using his wounded arm. Then the wind hit us broadsides and found in our high-piled lading a perfect target for attack. Oh, how slowly the islands, the promontories approached us!

Next Gaule told us he had water in his kayak. This was all we needed. By lucky forethought, though, it happened that I had taken a hose out of our first aid kit before we left and put it in Gaule's kayak, "just in case." So he then had the very dubious pleasure, every now and then, of sucking up and spitting out the water – salt water at that – from the bilge of his kayak.

In the dusk of midnight, we rounded the Hössliberg's southern tip and entered a fjord full of icebergs. This was the most difficult part. The icebergs were crammed together so closely that we had to twist now one way, now another, and quite often turn back altogether. Enormous icy roofs spread over some passages, large enough to shelter a hundred people, yet in reality ready to destroy all of them at once. Look at that ice wall that towers above us. Isn't it tilting now? We hear hollow thunder around us: collapsing icebergs. Now a clatter behind us: one of the roof overhangs that we had just passed.

We had been paddling for about nine hours incessantly, our hands more and more frozen and numbed, when the tent at the depot finally came in sight. According to Pastor Friedrichsen, the word *tuperk*, tent, and the expression for amazement, *tupinakrak*, come from the same root. The sight of a tent in this uninhabited land would therefore bring expressions of happy surprise from a Greenlander. Our feelings now concurred very much with this etymology. When we finally crawled out of our kayaks, we found that we could no longer stand on our feet, especially Gaule, who had been sitting deeper and deeper in icy water, despite the rubber hose, yet without a word of complaint.

Nothing had changed in the depot. In the boxes, everything was as I had packed it in Copenhagen the year before. What a strange feeling to see all these objects turn up again – even down to the soap and spare spectacles. At the time, I had packed these items up with the nagging thought that I might never see them again. For a while, it had seemed that all yesterday's doubts were rising once more out of these packings, like some miasma. But today's reality now helped to burn this feeling away.

For the next few days, our quartermaster Hössli consigned our ration book to the far corner of the tent. If there had been some festive wine in our depot, it would not have lasted long. Instead, we had to rely on the jams.

We planned to rest here for two days and keep the signal fires burning. If no Eskimos turned up, we would then continue the journey in our kayaks.

CHAPTER 10
TO ANGMAGSSALIK BY UMIAK

At noon on 31 July, we had taken shelter in the tent from the mosquitoes when, in the middle of a discussion on the beauty of Strasbourg's cathedral, we heard noises from the water and exclamations of amazement. It took me only a second to leap out of the tent: three kayaks were about to land! We fired shots of welcome and rushed down over the rocks with our smoking guns in hand.

They were already out of their kayaks: "Kanoripisi?" I ask, "ajungila?" How are you? Fine? For the time being, a broad "eeee" is all the answer I get. We soon find out that one Eskimo was named Ferdinand and the other one Timotheus, while the third one seemed not to admit to any name. Here we came to the end of the conversation. We climbed up to the tent and our new friends kept on muttering "Kujanak, kujanak" (We must be thankful). In the tent, I got out of them that they had come from their summer camp on Igdlitalik Island at the mouth of the fjord, roughly forty kilometres farther south, and that nobody was living any closer this year. So all our smoke and the fires had been in vain! It is not quite clear whether they were passing this place by chance or if they had been sent by Petersen.

Originally, I had intended to go ahead to Angmagssalik with Hössli and the Eskimos. However, Gaule's old infection had flared up again, and he didn't feel at all well. Under these circumstances, Hössli preferred not to leave him alone with Fick without a doctor. On 1 August, at 6 a.m. I therefore set out alone, accompanied by all the notebooks and two of the Eskimos, Ferdinand and the Nameless One.

For a while, I paddled in my own style and speed, and the Eskimos were courteous enough to go slowly. When they later offered a towing service, I gladly accepted. One tied his line to the bow of my kayak and the other one his bow to my stern, and thus we moved twice as fast despite the increased load. When we arrived at the other shore of the Sermilik Fjord around noon, I was serious when I asked them if it was not too tiring for them to tow me to Angmagssalik that same day. With a broad smile on their faces, they explained that they had been kayaking since they were children. They could easily do it. I felt so secure with them that I relaxed, only too happy no longer to have the responsibility. I ended up crawling down into my kayak and sleeping soundly. I only woke up from time to time when a piece of ice jolted the bow of the kayak or if I got thumped in the ribs through the thin skin of my boat, reminding me that, after all, I was still among the icebergs of the great Sermilik on the east coast and not in bed at home.

The trip still required every precaution, and I observed how much faster and better trained the Eskimos' eyes were than mine. Long before I had even noticed any movement, they would pull back the kayaks from a large ice block that was about to turn turtle in the water.

By 5 p.m., we were approaching a group of islands that loomed out of the fog at the mouth of the fjord where it joins the ocean. My Eskimos had indicated that this was where they had their tents. The Nameless One started to shout from afar: "Tigiput, tigi-pu-u-u-ut." They have come!

The high gables of the tents came into sight. People ran to the shore, women half-dressed, naked children, men dressed half in Greenlandic, half in European clothes, a strange mixture. There were piles of seal blubber on the shore. It wasn't easy to walk on the slippery greasy rocks.

I was led into Ferdinand's tent. His wife, Dora, was nursing little Andreas and at the same time tending an enormous blubber lamp with a wick at least half a metre wide. The tent was much statelier than the summer tents of the Western Greenlanders. There was a double wall of sealskin held up by a wooden framework; the big curtain of gut skin at the entrance was translucent. The plank bed on which I was invited to sit beside all the inhabitants was a good five metres long. At the other end of it lived another family. The sweetened condensed milk I had taken along won me the goodwill of the children and their mothers alike. But before they could offer me a gift of their own, which I feared would be seal blubber, I excused myself, and we travelled on in the kayaks to a second camp, where they said there was an *umiak*, a so-called women's boat. The owner, old Kitsigajak, immediately had it carried down from the rocks to the water. In no time, it was full of the women who were going to row, together with their little children. They made a special seat for me out of seal skins, and before I knew it, we were under way again.

Now there were no more icebergs to get in our way, only large slabs of sea ice. It was not always possible to avoid collisions, and they looked hazardous for our fragile boat. But they could stand more hard use than one might think. And any leak in the skin covering would immediately be sealed with blubber. By now we were following the sea coast northward, with the imposing rock precipices of the Orsuluviak on our left, like a marker guiding ships to the settlement. To the east were the fields of pack ice that make this coast so inaccessible.

A bay opened up inland, and over a small promontory, we saw three black wooden houses and a little church, and beside these, the low huts of the Eskimos. Angmagssalik!

My companions wanted to show off their "catch" and let me know that this was the moment to make myself seen, so I waved the flag and fired my gun in salute. At that, signs of life sprang up between the houses, with calls and shouts reverberating across the water. In the last rays of the sun, which was now sinking behind the northern ridges, the Danish flag rose up the flagpole. The sun could set now; it had seen enough and done its work for us.

On the shore, Petersen and the whole colony were waiting for us. He helped me out of the boat and took me right away to his house, where Mrs Petersen received me and led me to the washbasin with a friendly emphasis that I at first failed to understand. But one look in the mirror – for the first time in two months – revealed me literally as a brigand, albeit of a slightly good-natured mien (although some people might deny this).

I had brought mail for Petersen across the ice, two letters, the first in a year. He was crestfallen that there were not more. But who would have trusted me to make it?

My diary tells of a gourmet meal, fried eggs, coffee, salmon, and roast polar bear. And then I experienced a real bed. This was wonderful for the first night. Later, for many nights I could not stand sleeping in a house, and for a long time my comrades preferred to bed down in a sleeping bag on the hard floor. I had arrived on the first of August, our national holiday, a date that Stolberg had commended as being the most auspicious for a Swiss expedition. Early in the morning, when I stepped outside, a small gathering was assembled to inspect the unexpected guest from close up. The East Eskimos had, of course, heard from Petersen of our undertaking but did not believe such a thing was possible. And now these "denizens of the ice cap" had arrived after all!

On 2 August, two umiaks left for the Sermilik, and during the night of 4/5 August, they returned with my companions and all our gear, including the five dogs, which Petersen let us transfer to an uninhabited island.

CHAPTER 11

WITH THE EASTERN ESKIMOS

While we were waiting for the ship, expected early in September, we spent our time tying up all kinds of loose ends. Among others, there was the lengthy and successful excursion my companions undertook to collect anthropological data. Then we constructed a big sundial for Mr Petersen, whose local time was three-quarters of an hour off real time. I cannot imagine a better place for a sundial than this most inaccessible of human habitations.

There is really no other inhabited place in the whole world that is so totally cut off. To the west lies the ice cap never previously crossed. To the east is the offshore ice barrier that allows only one fleeting visit a year by a ship, if it can pass through the ice. That is Angmagssalik. I am afraid that I shall not really succeed in properly describing this little kingdom, a patriarchal society under the mild rule of the excellent Petersen. It would be a report from a different world. One would perhaps only remember ludicrous and trivial details, such as broad noses and blubber oil. We Central Europeans, sitting in our armchairs, are so convinced of our own worth that we are not able to take the East Eskimos seriously.

Anyone who has seen the Western Greenlanders is justified in believing that he has met an aboriginal people, although he may wish that he had been around two hundred years earlier, around the time of Hans Egede, when conditions were considerably less spoiled. Whoever meets the Eastern Greenlanders experiences exactly this backward leap in time.

I had known that there were supposed to be roughly four hundred Eskimos living in Angmagssalik and therefore expected a fairly large settlement. However, there were only four or five Eskimo huts standing beside the Danish buildings. Where were the others? I found out the answer the next day, a Saturday.

A whole flotilla came sailing into Tassiusak, as the Greenlanders call the settlement. I counted around twenty kayaks and five women's boats, umiaks, from which issued a stream of humanity. They all came from their camps located many hours away in the maze of islands. And they all had two reasons to make a visit before the fall storms and uncertain ice conditions would block the way: to visit the Danish store and attend church. The shop came first. On such days, good old Petersen is busy behind the scales from 5 a.m. until nightfall. Guns, powder, and shot are the most sought-after articles, then tools, European fabrics, and some grocery items. Everything is of good quality, some things even cheaper than at home. The item that customers ask for most is probably tobacco. Old Kitsigajak must have thought, "Nowadays they have it easy." In his day, he had to travel two thousand kilometres to buy tobacco, to South Greenland and back. And he did just that!

No alcohol, coffee, or bread is sold to the East Eskimos. The first is easy to understand, and a good thing. We might have chosen not to have kept the other two articles from them. But then, why teach them to use luxuries that are obviously of no benefit to them and foodstuffs that are hard to come by and they have not missed up to now?

The shopping over, camp for the night is quickly set up. They carry the umiaks on shore, turn them over, and there is a tent. When the bright blubber lamps are lit inside, the dark shadows of the people moving back and forth throw fantastic shadows on the boat's transparent skin. It is a captivating sight, and one that we never tired of watching.

The next day everybody went to church. There may have been two hundred people, including babes in arms. It so happened that the christening of several Eskimos took place that day. Among them was a grown-up heathen who was married right after the christening to, by Eskimo standards, a quite lovely bride. Next were a three-year-old girl and a baby who also had to "forsake the devil and his works," according to the age-old baptism ritual dating from the time of Charlemagne. When the woman responding for the baby did not answer the question about the devil right away, as she was busy attending to another of the baby's needs, the question was repeated immediately and emphatically.

Several weeks later when the ship arrived and the news of the death of the king of Denmark finally reached this place, a belated memorial service was held. It was probably asking a bit much of the Eastern Eskimos to show the appropriate sentiments, but I can still hear the rolling rhetoric of the native preacher's address ringing in my ears like hexameters.

The language of the Eastern Eskimo is, despite their geographical separation, remarkably similar to that of the Western ones. One might call it a less distinctly pronounced West Greenlandic. While the West enunciates clearly *ùvangà* (meaning "I"), on the east coast one hears a slurred *ù-a-à*.

There are indications that the Eastern Greenlanders parted from the other Eskimos in historical times near Smith Sound and migrated around the northern end of Greenland. Remains of settlements have been found on the northeast coast and farther south – for example, in Scoresby Sound. In some areas, these remains are so numerous that one might conclude that the east coast was at one time much more densely populated, if one did not take into account the nomadic lifestyle of the Eastern Eskimo. It seems strange to us that they are still nomadic now. An Eastern Eskimo is usually unable to tell you where his domicile is, only where he will be living this summer or this winter. Sometimes here, sometimes elsewhere. They do not necessarily move for a specific reason as, for example, to find better fishing grounds. It may happen that the boats of two families meet while they are on the move. One family moves for the winter to where the other one lived in summer, or vice versa, just because it pleases them to do so. Now I understand why nobody could predict whether we would meet people in the Sermilik Fjord.

There seemed to be a tendency for the Eastern Greenlanders to migrate gradually further south and around the south cape. One theory says that some Eastern Eskimos had reached the area of Godthaab even before the arrival of the Danes.

There is no doubt that the east coast would be depopulated by now if the Danish government had not founded the trading post of Angmagssalik in 1893. Now Greenlanders can sell their polar bear pelts there and do not have to travel so far south for their tobacco. The Danes have a fur monopoly, and they export over a hundred of these pelts from Angmagssalik every year, the only merchandise for export and therefore jealously guarded. This revenue pays for the station's upkeep but surely without much of a profit.

When we were there, unfortunately, no polar bears showed up, although some were shot near the settlements. There was too little sea ice left by then. However, we took Petersen's advice and never went any distance without a weapon.

I wasn't armed very effectively myself. I had only my signal rifle with its barrel like a cannon. If I put a good load of shot ahead of the cartridge – not exactly what the rifle was designed for – then such a recoil was to be expected that I awaited it at times with a secret horror. I was convinced that whatever flew out of the muzzle would be lethal enough even for a polar bear, should he come sufficiently close. And I was actually quite minded to let him get close enough.

Plate no. 32
Unidentified glacier calving into the sea, 1912.

Plate no. 33
"Old Kitsigajak," with traditional hairstyle, 1912.

Plate no. 34
The *Fox* in Ata Sound, with the Eqip Sermia glacier in the background, 1912.

Plate no. 35
Camp at the landing place in Ata Sound, 1912.

Plate no. 36
At Quervainshavn: de Quervain (*sitting above*),
Fick, Stolberg, Gaule, Mercanton, Jost, Hössli, and others, 1912.

Plate no. 37
The western party at their landing place in Ata Sound:
seated, Mercanton, Stolberg, and Jost, 1912.

Plate no. 38
Carrying supplies up to the ice cap: Jost, Fick, and Hössli, 1912.

Plate no. 39
Rocky foreland between the coast and the ice cap, 1912.

Plate no. 40
Crevasse zone: de Quervain is the right-hand figure, 1912.

Plate no. 41
Crevasse zone on the Eqip Sermia glacier, 1912.

Plate no. 42
Final camp before venturing onto the ice cap, 1912.

Plate no. 43
The supporting party turns back: *left to right*,
Gaule, Fick, Jost, Mercanton, Hössli, 1912.

Plate no. 44
Dog sledges with members of the supporting party, 1912.

Plate no. 45
Taking a break on the ice cap, Fick and Hössli, 1912.

Plate no. 46
Sledge dogs, 1912.

Plate no. 47
Elisabeth (Ella) de Quervain, visiting the Guithi family's tent at Angmagssalik, 1912.

Plate no. 48
Camping in stormy weather, with the sledge dogs snowed in, 1912.

Plate no. 49
Alfred de Quervain on the ice cap with anemometer, 1912.

Plate no. 50
Taking a break on the ice cap: *left to right*, Fick, de Quervain, Hössli, 1912.

Plate no. 51
Camping on the ice cap's crest: *left to right*, Hössli, Fick, Gaule, de Quervain, 1912.

Plate no. 52
De Quervain kayaking to Angmagssalik with Inuit escorts, 1912.

Plate no. 53
The “Nunatak des Suisses” on the ice cap’s western edge, 1912. Photo by Mercanton.

Plate no. 54

Family travelling in an umiak, the so-called women's boat, Angmagssalik, 1912.

Plate no. 55
Men at Angmagssalik, 1912.

Plate no. 56
Women at Angmagssalik, 1912.

Plate no. 57
Guithi's family and his brother in front of their summer tent, Angmagssalik, 1912.

Plate no. 58
Mother and child at Angmagssalik, 1912.

Plate no. 59
Children at Angmagssalik, 1912.

Plate no. 60
In the Guithi family's summer tent, Angmagssalik, 1912.

Plate no. 61
On the east coast: the island of Kekertatsuatsiak (*left*),
the "Gauleberg" (*right*), 1912.

Plate no. 62
Open country south of Angmagssalik, 1912.

But my resolve was never put to the test. Several times the dogs started to bark at night, and we were told that this was a sure sign that a bear was near. Otherwise, they would only howl. I ran out with my cannon, but by then everything was quiet again. If even I had caught hunting fever from my companions, so that I suffered from this temporary dearth of bears in Angmagssalik, how much more irksome must it have been for Fick, the hunter, to see no use for the beautiful rifle he'd lugged across the ice. We never heard more than the growling of the bear captured alive shortly before we arrived and now raging in his oaken cage.

At this time, the Eskimos on the east coast were still pure-blooded, which certainly is not the case on the west coast. They will probably remain so in the near future. But their special habits and customs are disappearing fast and will be lost in a few years' time.

The men used to wear their hair long, hanging free, tied by a leather thong around the foreheads. Now only some old men wear it the time-honoured way, either because they are unbaptized or because they don't want to bother themselves with the new fashion. They mix some European clothing with their own. Here the influence of the Greenlandic pastor's wife is clear to see. She introduced West Greenlandic dress, which led to an amusing misunderstanding among the women in their use of the undershirt. If a woman owns one of these luxury items, she will wear it over her fur pants, not inside. These originally pure white garments were too good to be hidden, but of course in normal use they don't stay white for long.

The summer tents are of an impressive size, but when you go inside, you rarely see any of the original soapstone cooking vessels, which were the rule only ten years ago. The store-bought blue enamel pots killed off the Stone Age on this coast in no time at all. And what is even more regrettable is that some overeager catechists from the orthodox seminary of Western Greenland have stilled the happy, innocent singing heard when the women's boats returned, and the drums that used to accompany a kayakman's song of triumph after a good hunt. No doubt Christianity, accepted in deep sincerity, has afforded great strength against the disastrous fear of the dead and the closely connected superstition of the stealing of souls, a belief of the old Angekoks. The murder and manslaughter that used to be an almost daily occurrence and were decimating the population, an outgrowth of this superstition, has stopped. But the drumming and singing should have been allowed to survive.

We soon came into some closer contact with the Eskimos. On the first night when we were all together again, side by side in our sleeping bags, a kayak messenger arrived after paddling for four hours from Cape Dan, to ask if the doctor could come and see the wife of the catechist, who was seriously ill. Again,

I was amazed to see how quickly the Eastern Eskimos can make themselves ready for travel. At the time, there were not many people on hand in the colony, yet within a quarter of an hour, a full crew for a women's boat arrived at the beach. Two minutes later we were under way, with, above all, the precious doctor, myself as translator from German to Danish, and the half-Greenlander Chemnitz for translating Danish to Greenlandic. It was a wondrous voyage under the dusky night sky, into which we saw the moon rising from behind the mountains. We had almost forgotten it existed.

Hössli succeeded in calming the first patient and giving her the necessary medicine. There was another case, much worse. A man who had broken his thigh a year before was forced to lie motionless on his stomach. "Tokuvà?" he groaned. Do I have to die? Despite all our efforts, he could not be helped. I was at his funeral two weeks later. There was no ceremony, for he had died a heathen. His wife, wavering fearfully between the old and the new faiths, asked if it would harm her if she touched the body.

We became quite friendly with three brothers who had moved their communal tent and their families to the vicinity of Angmagssalik, as one wife was taking instruction at the pastor's for her christening. They had already started to build a house for the winter, proof that these christenings are taken seriously. We often visited with Guithi in his tent. The three mothers would sit silently, with great dignity, on the long platform in front of their blubber lamps, tending them or looking after the children who lay at the rear of the platform, scarcely disturbing the peace. We never heard a vehement word, even between adults. We could not, of course, contribute significantly to the conversation. The inhabitants of the tent invited us in and welcomed us with their friendly smiles, and we in turn tried to do likewise, and after about half an hour we took our leave with an especially broad smile. Every now and then, we enlivened the scene by a little bartering, but I did not even try to acquire any of their antique possessions. I really did not have the heart to accelerate what I knew would happen anyway, the disappearance of their traditional implements.

I believe the expedition left a pretty good impression with the younger generation, too, because we took part in their games. Fick and Gaule excelled in gymnastics, while Hössli no doubt left a lasting mark by introducing some games that had been the joy of his youth, not so long ago. I wonder if the East Eskimos still play Gis, or Yellow Fox. Maybe they changed the yellow to blue, in keeping with their polar colours.

A topic looming large in the conversation of the colony was the question of when the ship would arrive. The Petersens were less eager to see her than one would have expected: they still had a backlog of letters to write. Above all, we hoped that it would be the *Godthaab*, but if she hadn't returned soon enough from Koch's expedition to the northwest coast, then it would be a Norwegian ship. Our ingenious calculations said that she could not arrive before 1 September under any circumstances, because otherwise she could not have any consignments from Copenhagen on board (one of which, I vaguely hoped, would be my wife). We planned to post a lookout on the hill from 29 or 30 August onwards.

However, on 28 August, the clouds were hanging low, and we were in no hurry to get up when the Greenlandic nurse, who looked after patients and the expedition's kamiks, rushed in with "Umiarssuit!"

It could not be, but it was. The *Godthaab* was gliding around the promontory into Tassiusak Bay. I quickly hoisted the flag in front of our little house. While my companions stood and stared, I ran to the bay and took my kayak, as the boats could not be launched so quickly at low tide. There was no chance now that my wife could be on board, but the mail was worth the hurry.

How wrong I was!

On the ship, the tension had been great. Were the expeditioners here? The Eskimos overflowed with pleasure at the new guest. Only catechist Ohlsen and his friends lamented that it was only my wife and not the Western Greenlander bride whom they had expected. The ship brought good news from all our families, but also a sad message: Professor F.A. Forel, the expedition's patron, had died. Thus the storm on the ice cap had known better when it ripped Mercanton's letter to Forel out of my hand; and when I named Mount Forel, it was already a monument to the deceased.

On 3 September, we waved goodbye to Petersen and his wife, who had been so kind to us, and to everybody else in Angmagssalik. In the end, we had to leave our dogs behind, as the captain had been given strict orders in Copenhagen not to let them on board, and there was nothing we could do. I felt like a traitor leaving them there, and even now, I can't rid myself of a certain resentment against this edict.

Our good friend Guithi came once more from his summer camp and shed warm tears. My companions are not sentimental men, but they watched with emotion as the coast disappeared forever from our sight. This land had captured our thoughts, and they would return there again and again. Is it just this particular stretch of country? I do not think so. Others may feel the same about other places. To us Greenland was a wondrous revelation.

Among the insights we – or at least I myself – gained is an awareness that the maxims that our civilization take for granted, namely, "faster and faster" and "more and more," have in fact made fools of us. Do we believe that the quality of our lives is improved tenfold by going ten times as fast, or by hearing and doing ten times as much every day? What if the value of our impressions turns out to be correspondingly superficial as they grow more fleeting? What do we win?

One might object that in the end we have nothing to lose. One times ten or ten times one is all the same. Well, I wonder if that is really the case.

For we have now arrived at a limit beyond which the immutable laws of our being will always have their way. That is, if sensations reach us ten times faster, their impression will diminish tenfold, with the result that the faster we live, the more impoverished we will become. That is a small truth I have learned from the ice cap, from the midnight sun and the hundreds of little wrinkles in old Kitsigajak's face. It is another of the results of the expedition that I may not suppress.

CHAPTER 12
RETURN VIA ICELAND: SCIENTIFIC RESULTS

The *Godthaab* would take us to Iceland. A stormy northeasterly kept us from docking in Reykjavik, the capital with all its tin-roofed houses, until 8 September in the evening. The first thing we did was to send messages home of the expedition's safe arrival. The next day we received a congratulatory telegram from the Schweizerische Naturforschende Gesellschaft and from the Danish authorities. But we still had to wait another two weeks for a ship to the continent. This involuntary stay gave us an opportunity to get acquainted with the surroundings and the people, on horseback and of course in the rain.

What we saw and experienced obviously calls for a comparison with Greenland. The vegetation in the Icelandic valleys is little different from that of Greenland's fjords. Icelandic farmers have to wrest every foot of grass from their slopes of scree just as, long ago, their vanished predecessors in Greenland had to struggle against nature. The Norse settlements in Greenland must have looked very similar to the Icelandic farmsteads of today. But how differently the modern inhabitants of these two countries have responded to the same harsh natural conditions.

The Greenlandic hunter, untrammelled by civilization, has found an equilibrium with nature. His few possessions satisfy him and he can afford to laugh and befriend the stranger as well.

The Icelander, descended from the Norsemen of old and self-appointed saviour and guardian of European culture, is weighed down by the double burden of wresting a living from the uncooperative soil and keeping the old culture alive. He has become dour and embittered. These are an upright and proud people. The women all carry themselves as if each one were the queenly Brunhilde whom Gunther wooed in far-off Iceland long ago. But they are unfriendly, reticent, almost petrified in look and thought, as if they were directed both backward to Iceland's past glories and at the same time forward to the time when the Icelandic falcon will once again soar aloft, free of the hated Danish cage. This is their dream, their obsession and passion. And this is the goal that the best of them are working for.

We did not suffer from an excess of Icelandic amiability. As a parting salutation, they stuck my wife and myself into a dark and airless hole on the ship – possibly in acknowledgment of my Greenlandic training – compared with which the cabin on the *Godthaab* had been quite comfortable. While we sat reading in the ship's salon, some young Icelandic ladies and gentlemen gave us a measure of their civility by simply pulling the tablecloth for their card game from under our books. All night there was such noise and uproar in their cabins that we would have preferred three whole Eskimo families as neighbours to these scions of the Norse. They really could learn some courtesy from the Danes, to whom they have felt so superior since the days of the Edda.[1]

Early on 29 September, our steamer *Sterling* docked in Copenhagen. Few people were up so early to greet the boat from Iceland. Was somebody waving something red at us? It was a Swiss flag, and the person waving it must be Mme Mercanton, together with her husband. The last person we'd left on the west coast of Greenland was now the first to greet us on the continent. We could not have wished for a more cheerful reception.

My stay in Copenhagen almost started with a police fine. When Mercanton asked about weapons, I unthinkingly fired off our East Greenland signal gun, not at first understanding why he was so horrified at my gesture. In Greenland, tipping your hat and shooting a rifle were one and the same thing, but Mercanton had obviously been domesticated again.

I too soon had reason to feel rather civilized when I met a gathering of top hats. These were worn by a delegation from the Royal Danish Geographical Society, who were waiting for us at the hotel. Their speaker received me with a solemn little speech, of which the most I can remember is the end of the pencil I must have been twisting around in my fingers, rather embarrassed by it all. Then we were invited to a "little dinner" at the Geographical Society, and a similar invitation came from the Swiss Club. We were happy that our first visitors were the director of the colonies in Greenland, Carl Ryberg, and Commander Holm, who

1 The Norse epic (EQS).

had both been so interested in our undertaking and so helpful. Our old friend, the writer Dr Norman Hansen, brought a copy of his Greenland novel *I Jöklens Favn*, fresh off the press as a first greeting on our return. Our Swiss compatriots in Copenhagen, whose main interest is not usually polar research, organized a very enjoyable party for us. It was reassuring to me to think that an accomplishment even in an "unproductive" scientific field by a Swiss party is at least perceived to do credit to the nation in general. But to say that ideas are more concrete than material success – who would dare to invert the normal order like this?

Our reception at Denmark's Royal Geographic Society was no less cordial, and above all, we were honoured to meet almost all the men who had contributed to the exploration of the north. There was J.A.D. Jensen, the first to venture onto the ice cap; Gustav Holm, who had undertaken the first survey of the east coast; Count Moltke and Garde, who had made the longest expedition in the south after Nansen; Steenstrup, Hammer, and Engell; and also Captain Mikkelsen, still gaunt from his two-year ordeal on Greenland's northeastern coast. That all these experts in the field thought highly enough of our endeavours to greet us made up for many an awkward moment. They also delighted us by placing little Swiss flags on the table. For this reason, we were happy that the king received the leader of the expedition in an audience. He was also kind enough to think of honouring me, as the expedition's representative, with the Order of the Dannebrog. I had to advise him, of course, that the Swiss constitution would not allow me, as a functionary of the state, to accept it.

"But why this expedition? What's the use of all this?" We have heard this question so often that I cannot simply let it pass. Of course, the people who alone have the right to ask, those who actively helped us, have probably already found the answer to this question.

The polar explorations of past centuries were launched for commercial reasons, namely to open a northwest passage around America and Asia for trade. And such motives certainly dominated the golden age of discovery. It is hardly necessary to add that these aims seemed to be well grounded. At the time, the explorers simply took what they thought was their due and then some.

The present age is no less interested in practical results than was the past. In the exploration of the earth, and this is what we are talking about, a prevailing opinion is that the so-called lords of creation should seek to know their realm as a matter of principle, whether this knowledge has any practical application or not, and such a viewpoint is accepted in the field of polar research too. This is the scientific point of view. Some may object to it. (Actually most people do, though they make an exception for the "practical sciences," thus trying to reap where they did not sow.) Yet, whoever thinks in this way will never be satisfied by the results of our expedition.

There are two different streams in scientific polar exploration. One, historically and in the popular view the primary one, has the purpose of opening up hitherto unknown areas. The second, following closely behind, seeks to deepen our knowledge of the natural history of these regions by systematic research, preferably at well-established observation posts. There are scientific disciplines in which each man can be left to work according to his temperament and where his positive advances are acknowledged. Unfortunately, we see again and again that these two streams are unreasonably played against each other.

Only a few years ago, an expedition's achievements were often measured, unjustly, only by the distance it covered. Today, those hurling themselves toward the poles hear the equally unfair reproach of having done nothing for science because they cannot produce mean monthly temperatures for each of their campsites. But as long as there is a passage through the still unknown regions of the earth, the noblest task of the earth sciences is to walk these paths in order first of all to establish the earth's topography.

We were fortunate to work, within our modest means, in both these directions. This is neither the place nor the time to enter into specific details of the work and the results we achieved. The evaluation of the measurements still requires considerably more time.

We have established a new profile across the seven-hundred-kilometre breadth of the island of Greenland, the longest and most accurate to date. The positions are, on the average, accurate to one-tenth of a minute (of arc) in latitude, and two to three seconds (of time) in longitude. The altitude readings would usually allow an accuracy of few metres. In this case, there was much less uncertainty in working them out, a process that always has a strong influence on such measurements, thanks to the favourable selection of the profile from between two surveyed base stations on the coast. Apart from our crossing, there exists only one other complete profile of the inland ice cap. As the ice cap is one of the most interesting formations on the surface of the earth, this profile is not simply a cross-section through just any unexplored region of the world but represents a new archetype. It has an additional feature of interest. The profile crosses the route of two previous forays onto the ice cap (Peary's and Nordenskjöld's), whose topographic data did not really agree with each other. We eliminated these contradictions with measurements of unassailable quality. The final profile will differ very little from the preliminary one shown here.

This cross-section confirms first of all the assumption that the central region is completely covered with ice. A different scenario – for example, the oases conjectured by Nordenskjöld – was no longer tenable after Nansen's crossing, although I did not reject the idea of mountain massifs possibly breaking through. Nansen had already guessed that later expeditions would find that the ice cap flattened out farther north. We were able to confirm this, contrary to theories that called for a considerably higher profile farther north. However, we do make the important qualification that the inland ice does not drop off toward the northeast but, on the contrary, rises higher. According to the results of our crossing, the highest altitudes on the ice cap will be found not in the south but in a northerly direction, possibly between our highest point and the area around Scoresby Sound. These regions of the ice cap, where the ice also shows different characteristics in relation to the coastal area as compared with the west coast, should be the goal of a next expedition. It is obvious that one must expect surprises there, as the southern spur, the mountain range including Mount Forel, has shown. At 2,760 metres, this elevation is considerably higher than the highest point on the ice cap. We have measurably increased our knowledge of the physical and meteorological conditions of the ice cap by our careful observations, which were executed in a different season from those of the first crossing. Our observations concerned the melting zone, the extent of the crevassed areas, precipitation, wind conditions, and temperatures, and partly also the magnetic phenomena, which evinced strange anomalies that might be explained by the underlying basalt. The graph reproduced here shows the temperature variations during the crossing. The difference between the small daily variations in the rim zone and the large variations and the low temperatures in the central area are obvious. In summer, the cold air of the central plateau flows like water from the high plains in all directions, although shifted to the right by the earth's rotation.

All these observations will be of special interest for the imminent Danish crossing in northern Greenland. Then it will be possible to draw a first approximate topographical map of the interior of Greenland.[2]

The work of the western party under Professor Mercanton complements the meteorological observations of our profile. The party made numerous measurements, primarily of the ice movements and the topography of the rim area of the ice cap near our departure point, which the traversing group would never have been able to do alone. In another field, our anthropological measurements

2 At the time of printing, I received news of the successful crossing, which confirms our expectations; they found altitudes of between 2,500 and 3,000 metres (AdQ).

and collections added some welcome information, especially about the usually inaccessible east coast. The data on the craniums of the pure Eskimo race are particularly valuable and are already being evaluated elsewhere.

I especially want to mention the series of aerological measurements made in conjunction with parallel observations at stations in Iceland and Spitzbergen, which complete our earlier measurements. These were made by Dr Jost and Dr Stolberg, who stayed all winter on Disko Bay in West Greenland. They were very successful.

Their observations, from a total of 120 weather balloon launches, provided the important information that, even in winter, there is no uniform polar vortex, even at higher altitudes.

Finally, let us remember the personal rewards that the members of the expedition brought back with them. Certainly not pecuniary ones, for leaders of expeditions, whether big or small, and despite all the interest that they may create, must be happy if they manage to pay off all their debts. I think rather of the imperishable experiences and perspectives we won, which will last us a lifetime and may in time stimulate and inspire others. I think also of that sense of unfettered freedom and uplift, not often attainable at home, that derives from directing one's mental and physical resources totally and harmoniously to a single goal. This gives one a feeling of exaltation rather than of superiority or conceit. As one is made so much aware of the limits of one's own powers in the face of far greater forces, mere pride could never be the ultimate emotion prompted by our success. But we are grateful to accept that success and to offer it in return as an expression of thanks to all those who helped us.

THE SUMMER OF THE WESTERN PARTY

PAUL-LOUIS MERCANTON

Evening, 22 June. So here we are. Our small western party, Dr Stolberg, Dr Jost, and I, have settled in at the rim of the inland ice sheet. Stolberg had taken great pains to find this sheltered spot, which gave us some protection against the fury of the storm that almost shredded our tent last night. Just this morning, Jost and I wished bon voyage to our brave companions of the eastern party, eighteen kilometres from here at one thousand metres altitude, totally surrounded by the ice sheet. The flag with the white cross fluttering over the small dark tent, the loaded sleds, and the dogs saluted us one last time. I waved back with my little Vaudois flag, given to me by the Société Vaudoise de Sciences Naturelles, and so we parted.

It was with a heavy heart that we saw the four familiar figures disappear behind the snowy horizon. What wouldn't we have given at that moment to share their labours and their dangers, and of course their success! Of their success, we are sure. We have faith in the careful preparations for the undertaking, and we trust the leader's competence. Don't they also owe it to the honour of the country? They must succeed.

We quickly retraced the stretch of the last two days' marches, and with compass and barometer took the general topographical measurements of the route. This is one of the jobs that we will have to continue down to the shore. On the way up, de Quervain could not spare the time for these observations.

The two Greenlanders, Jens and Emil, are relieved of their secret worries about the big glacier and are very happy to be heading for home. Today, shod in the new kamiks that de Quervain had handed out, they were cheerfully trotting behind us over the bumpy ice, which became progressively rougher in the hot sun.

Soon the rounded knoll of the Ilulialik nunatak, our guidepost on the way up to the ice sheet, rises over the horizon. (Isolated rock massifs in the rim zone which are entirely surrounded by ice are called *nunataks*, newly appearing land, by the Eskimos.) Sometimes, as in this case, the name also applies to big outcrops of rock that face the ocean on one side. At the first campsite, we pick up our packs again, which have not become lighter with the cryoconite material that we had collected.

A short stop, a pemmican snack, and on we go. Our faces hurt from the reflected glare of the ice. We jump over crevasses and run down the slope of the great moraine. This takes us five and a half hours for the twenty kilometres. We have reached the depot.

After resting briefly, we lug our movable home to the station with the help of the Greenlanders who will leave us tomorrow. "The station" is what we call our new camp, and rightly so, because our tent will be set up here for five weeks. Just beside it is the Greenlanders' tent, which will serve as storage shed and as guest room for the occasional visiting Greenlanders.

The plans for my own glaciological studies have had to be subordinated to a certain degree to the aims of the main expedition. Beside the continuing observation of the varied manifestations of the surrounding glacier world, I plan measurements of the movement of the inland ice sheet as follows:

First: in an area of the front where the melting of the ice masses takes place on relatively level ground.

Second: in the immediate vicinity of a nunatak that holds up the fiow, similar to a bridge pier in a river.

Third: where the ice sheet breaks off into the sea.

Earlier, I had secretly hoped that we would be able to work close to the Reindeer nunatak in the area of the Karajak glacier. However, we reached the inland ice in a different area and had to give up that plan, but we did find the desired conditions here too. One tongue of the ice sheet extended as far as the Nunap Kigdlinga, where we were located, and was therefore perfect for work on the first project.

There was also the exposed ridge of a massive nunatak barely twenty-five kilometres north of the station, rising up between two steep ice streams. When we had made our reconnaissance on 14 June, de Quervain, Jost, and I had decided that this would be an ideal nunatak for a glaciologist and that it would not be overly difficult to reach. However, we could see the seracs[1] in the crevasses of

1 Blocks or sharp ridges of ice formed in the crevasses of glaciers.

the two adjoining glaciers stretching far into the ice sheet, so that we wondered if it would not be easier to reach it from the sea, starting at the big nunatak. I seriously considered returning to Quervainshavn to try to reach our "base of operation" by boat. But then what would happen to our first project on the program, the only one whose success was assured? For this, we were set up here, and besides, the front of the Eqip Sermia was a good area for item three on our program. "A bird in the hand is better than two in the bush" was my decision. If the weather would cooperate a little, we hoped to reach the nunatak in the time between our two series of observations on the main project.

We had a six-week time span ahead of us. Of this, we had to set aside several days for the topographical survey of the Nunap Kigdlinga and, above all, of Quervainshavn, both part of the expedition's route. The return to the inhabited areas at the end of August would also take quite some time, as we had a lot of baggage to transport. In addition, bad weather, mosquitoes, and strong winds were responsible for shortening our valuable time in spite of all our painstaking efforts.

I shall try to describe the surroundings of our temporary home. The station was situated about eight hundred metres from the ice edge at an altitude of 535 metres. We had set up the station on a narrow rocky ridge at the side of a small hill, relatively well protected from the endless foehn storms. To the south, a grassy ledge led gently down to a small lake that was fed by water from a snowy slope nearby. To the west was a stony ravine ending in a treacherous drop. In the distance, through a narrow gap, we could see the glimmering blue waters of the Ata Sound with its icebergs. Behind the dark slopes of Igdloluarsuit Island to the east appeared the white strip of the mighty Torsukatak ice fjord, and the horizon was completed by the walls of Nugsuak and the distant peaks of the mountains on Disko.

On the northern horizon lay the ice sheet, partly obscured by the huge Ilulialik nunatak, and in this direction too rose up "our" nunatak. A little closer, the mighty Eqip Sermia ice stream broke off into the sea. When the midnight sun in the cloudless sky bathed the ice sheet in a pale gold, it looked like a sea of frozen waves, a vision of unbelievable beauty.

Unfortunately, we did not manage to find a spot for our tent (which was of a similar construction to de Quervain's) that was totally sheltered from the wind. Consequently, we had to grapple again and again with the prevailing southeasterly winds.

When the equipment for the western party was chosen, one main consideration was weight, because we would have to rely on the strength of our own backs to carry everything. We had expected to be isolated and frequently on the move. But how could our esteemed leader have been of the opinion that the western party, the coastal, field, and rock group, would live under a permanently blue sky, continuously enjoying the luxurious advantages of civilization? This remains a mystery. We know for sure that our tent, made of raw silk and translucent, was delightful in good weather, but in rain and wind – I call on the stoical Stolberg to testify that with the anemometer he twice measured a wind speed of 0.5 metres a second in the closed tent, at the spot where his head was in vain trying to find some restful slumber. Even so, we loved our silken shelter very much.

We can't say the same for our sleeping bags, the fiendish devisings of a German industrialist, DRGM.[2] I prefer to keep his actual name secret, the name on which we heaped a thousand of the most horrific curses while we were on the ice. The bags were made of a supposedly waterproof porous material, lined with flannel wrapped around air cushions. Hooks and buttons, badly sewn on, were supposed to close up the contraption, but one's shoulder remained outside, exposed to wind and weather. The cushions offered two possibilities: at best and in rare cases, the air stayed in, but one had to remain stretched out like a mummy in a coffin. If the sleeper tried to find another position, the cushion stuck to his back, tipping him onto the hard floor. Or, the cushion collapsed right away and the owner was free to find some fleeting sleep in any position he liked. We had to sleep in our clothes, of course. On the ice, these bags just were not serviceable enough.

Let this be a warning to future explorers, if they haven't already learned enough from the eastern party's praise for their fur sleeping bags. [Note by de Quervain: Fur sleeping bags would not actually have suited the conditions in the rim zone. The type that is criticized here had proved themselves quite well three years earlier on the ice sheet. We could not foresee the miserable quality of the bags subsequently delivered.]

Our first task, even before putting up the tent, was to set up the meteorological observation post. Stolberg and Jost were responsible for the observations, not always an easy job. They took turns with eagerness and perseverance, undaunted by the harsh nights or the fiendish mosquitoes; with equanimity, they read off the air temperature and humidity from the aspirated thermometer, measured the wind speed with the anemometer, or observed the forever-changing forms of the clouds. A little flag on a bamboo pole fluttering in the stiff wind gave the wind direction.

2 Deutsche Reichs-Gebrauchsmuster: equivalent to a trademark for German products up to 1945.

We were supplied with ample food provisions: we had no fear of death by starvation. The amount of rye bread, which we called "cannon shot," was simply overwhelming. There were ample supplies of pemmican, zwieback rusks, and crispbread, milk and honey too, as well as chocolate, canned vegetables, and fruit. But where were the biscuits? And where was the bacon that the eastern party so generously left for us? *Imaka kimit*? Maybe the dogs?

One slip of the eastern party could have had serious consequences for us. All the small fine wire holders to clean any plugged nozzles of the Primus cookers were on their way to Angmagssalik. Had we not found one in the refuse from the final camp, and if my friend Jules Jacot-Guillarmod, the Himalaya explorer, had not as a prescient precaution – praise and thanks to him – slipped a length of steel wire into my baggage, we really would have been in trouble.

Furthermore, our friends, in their haste to depart, had left several unneeded items in various places along the Nunap Kigdlinga. These we had to collect as part of our program. All summer long, a rejected sledge stuck in the rocks of the "Bad Step," lifting its runners to heaven in mute protest.

Quite often – too often, indeed – we had to descend to the main depot at Quervainshavn. Our spare food supplies and instruments, our clothes and kayaks were there, not to forget the *Ella*, whose seaworthiness dwindled day by day. This unhappy boat, for which we had held such high hopes, had become a real nuisance. To keep her from being battered by the drifting ice slabs, we at first pulled her up on the beach. But the hot June sun made a useless sieve out of her, whereupon we put her back in the water in a quiet bay of the fjord. Alas, she then became a toy of the tides and the foehn winds, and one day we found her badly mauled, wrecked at low tide on some pointed stones, without her benches and with a hole in her bottom. Poor *Ella*! We later fixed her up enough for her to be towed as far as Jakobshavn, where she has remained ever since.

At first, we were tempted to start our work at grassy Quervainshavn, but right away, on our first visit on 24 June, we found that this would be impossible. Despite the late hour, the bloodthirsty mosquitoes were there in countless numbers. It didn't help to escape onto the water; there were even more of them there! I'll never forget how we made the altitude measurements that night; but then we had similar experiences when measuring the solar elevation at our station.

We had hoped that the immediate vicinity of the inland ice sheet would keep the harassing mosquitoes at a respectful distance. How naïve. The next morning *Culex nigripes* swarmed around our station, more persistent than ever. So, for the days ahead, to the end of July, our choices outside the tent were to be blown away by the foehn, to be soaked by all the waters of heaven, or to have our living bodies sucked empty by mosquitoes. Obviously, these are not the best conditions for work in the open air. On one occasion, these beasts pursued us right onto the ice sheet. As soon as the wind drops or the rain eases, they fly out in swarms from behind every patch of lichen and every tuft of grass to batten on us *par l'odeur alléchés* – drawn by the enticing scent, to quote Lafontaine. I remember how a mosquito once drew blood by quickly stinging the hand with which I wanted to slap the others from my forehead.

The cool days of August somewhat alleviated our suffering, for *Simulium vittatum*, the "stupid mosquito," as the Greenlanders call it, which emerges at that time, isn't as vicious as *Culex nigripes*. At least it leaves behind no irritant toxin when it draws our blood.

I mentioned wind and rain. I must also add snow, which three times blanketed the surrounding area in a white coat. In the summer of 1912, both Greenland and Europe had an exceptional number of rainy days. From the end of June to the end of July, it rained at our station one day out of three on average. And the wind-free days we could count on the fingers of one hand. The southeasterly wind blew almost without interruption at an average speed of eight metres a second, and often at ten metres a second, on 21 July even at 18.1 metres a second, and this though our station was in a relatively sheltered place. On the great moraine, we measured as much as 20.1 metres a second (72 kilometres an hour). Under these circumstances, Jost, who was to take pictures with the large 13 by 18 camera, had no easy task. Once when I loosened the clamp, I found that the telescope swivelled like a weathervane, and the wind blew me to the ground twice near the moraine wall where we had set up the instrument.

The temperature hovered around 5°C. All summer long, the sky was rather unusual. A fine white veil of cirrus clouds masked the blue of the sky and weakened the sun's rays. The blood-red sun stood low over the northern horizon, reminding us that summer would soon be over. Some poor little flowers bloomed at our feet among the sparse lichens and mosses and in the cracks between the rocks. Bushes were no longer in evidence, as if we were at 2,600 metres in the Alps. I had brought some cacti from Europe, and for weeks I looked after them in their little box, but this was not enough to conjure up a tropical vegetation. Compared with this place, Quervainshavn was a real Garden of Eden, but without any tree of knowledge. There the cassiope, sedum, and vaccinium bloomed in profusion, and the alpine rhododendron painted carmine spots on the dense green moss spread like a soft carpet under our feet. Dwarf birches hugged the smooth gneiss with their branches in order to soak up all the sun's rays. *Salix glauca*, a willow with velvety light-green leaves, managed to grow even to a man's height when protected from the wind by boulders.

There were almost no animals. Only ptarmigan were abundant, and near the fjord, all sorts of gulls. Occasionally, one or the other ended up in our cooking pot. I was very lucky to bag a pair of snow ducks (*Harelda hiemalis*) at the shore of a lake. I felt a little conscience-stricken at ending their idyllic existence, but the delicious meal soon quelled our bad consciences. After a stubborn chase, Jost shot a snow hare that had teased him from close by when he had no weapon at hand. Both of us also got an arctic fox, but not even Jost, zealous hunter as he was, managed to shoot one of the many seals that of an evening poked their heads out of the fjord, always just too far away. However, the Greenlanders generously shared their catches with us, even their fish.

They often came to visit, whole umiaks full, and helped us to carry our gear. Some hunters came from Ata or Arsivik out of curiosity or hoping for a little paid work. As is the custom in Switzerland, we treated the Greenlanders as friends and equals and never regretted it. They willingly did our transport and carried messages or letters without fail.

Best of all, two of the most able men from Ata, the catechist Gabriel Knudson, our "Gaba," and the hunter Emmanuel Lange, stayed with us, sometimes at the station, sometimes at Quervainshavn. They shared our bread and helped us in a hundred small ways, and with their kayaks they were our link to the civilized world. Jost, broad-shouldered and strong, inspired such trust that Emmanuel one day plucked up the courage to let himself be lowered by him into a crevasse of the Eqip Sermia to retrieve my ice axe.

In the end, we received a letter of thanks for our good conduct, addressed to the Katsisortormiut nalagarsuit (the Supreme Council of the land of the high mountains), which translates as follows:

> This summer, on 9 June 1912, members of the expedition reached the inland ice sheet and the Greenlanders loved them, because they were like the Danes; we thank the Supreme Council of Switzerland for having sent us these brave men, and we thank the travellers for having been so good to the Greenlanders. For this, we have a high regard for the expedition. And I ask the Supreme Council to believe that we have treated the expedition well, although it was not Danish.
>
> Arsivik, 16 August 1912
> Niels Magnusson

Oh, innocent children of the Arctic! These large parties, although a very pleasant diversion, became wearisome after a while. Our supplies felt their effect, particularly since Jost tended to spoil the good people.

When we were alone, we followed the same dietary policies as our companions on the inland ice. We possibly had more choice in our menus, but then we had fewer creature comforts, for, unfortunately, all the ground coffee and cocoa powder had disappeared across the ice into the distant east. Who can reproach us for losing so much time scraping up Lindt chocolate with a knife and roasting coffee on the cover of a tin over the Primus stove?

After a good breakfast, we went to work. Mostly we used the night hours that we extended at will, depending on the vagaries of the weather. On returning, we recharged ourselves for the rest of the day with a strong pemmican soup. What a dinner! Rich, hot, salty, spiced with Maggi, and with added canned vegetables, as long as they lasted. After the third bowl one felt an irresistible urge to nap or smoke a well-deserved pipe. Tea quenched our burning thirst after the salty meal. Never did I feel better than on this diet of fresh air and pemmican.

If it rained, we stayed in the tent in our so-called waterproof sleeping bags, without taking off either our anoraks or kamiks. Propping our heads up on our personal baggage piled up in the apse of the tent, we listened to varied tales from our veteran Greenland expeditioner Stolberg, or we read from the "good books" in our library, a truly eclectic choice of works. Dr W. Jordan's *Tables for Position-Fixing* rubbed shoulders with Tristan Bernard's *Memoires d'un jeune homme rangé*, and *Faust* with *Pantagruel*, while *The Ice Age* by Dr Emil Werth stood beside *Le modernisme bouddhiste* by Mme Alexandra David. Often I also had the tedious but necessary job of transcribing the previous evening's observations, while Jost mended his fur pants and Stolberg brewed up a beverage to console us.

On 8 July, a remarkable day, Gaba and three friends finally brought the long-delayed mail: some ninety-seven letters and half a dozen parcels, among them three pots of delicious honey, the tender gesture of a fatherly professor of physics for Jost, which the rest of us could share, of course. What joy! We offered the bearers a banquet and then fell to devouring our letters. There was not much of interest in the newspapers; even the *Gazette de Lausanne*, I admit, held little attraction for me. We were too far away from the centre of attention.

Our joy was dimmed, however, by the news that the old *Fox* had run aground near Agto and was beyond repair. We had become quite fond of the gallant little ship and her crew. On a rock ledge at Quervainshavn, we erected a monument in her honour by setting up an old hydrogen flask with an inscription.[3] Moreover,

3 Marcel de Quervain saw this "monument" in June 1959, the only trace of the expedition still extant (EQS).

the wreck of the *Fox* had serious consequences for us. Our group would have to leave earlier than planned from here, since I, the leader of the group, had to return to Europe, no matter what.

As soon as we were settled, we got down to work on the first section of our program. We really regret that we cannot give a more detailed description of the rocky terrain of the Nunap Kigdlinga, the point where we started our work. After two months in the area, this interesting rock formation became very familiar and dear to us. Let me try to sketch it by enlarging on some remarks de Quervain made.

Imagine an enormous triangular rock massif with sides ten kilometres long. The easternmost of these sides bounds the front of the ice sheet at an altitude of 550 to 600 metres. On it rests the huge moraine, eight kilometres wide, the wall that the eastern party had to cross. The ice abuts this rock massif on both sides, the massive ice stream of the Eqip Sermia to the north, and the southern glacier Sermerk Kujadlek with a more modest spur to the south. It would be hard without a precise map to give a satisfactory description of the variety of lakes, watercourses, gorges, and valleys that mark the surface of the Kigdlinga.

For us, though, several of these played a big role, impeding our progress, particularly those by the names of Kororsuak (big valley), Koropiluk (bad gorge), and the "bad step." Many a heavily loaded member of the eastern and western party sweated profusely there, and the glances that measured these steep slopes and the lake shores always asked: how much further? The outlets of all these lakes of the high plateau finally flow into the little valley of the Eqip Kungua to reach the bay formed by the Eqip Sermia, the place to which the officers of the *Fox* gave the name Quervainshavn. From there we finally worked out a path to the inland ice sheet that avoided the worst obstacles and took us three and a half hours to walk.

While Stolberg and Jost first reconnoitred the above-mentioned southern glacier, whose seracs could be seen at the end of Kororsuak, I finally found that the most suitable point for the basis of the triangulation of the inland ice sheet was the rim of the rocky plateau where the eastern party had started their trek.

We had great difficulties in marking out the base, and we pushed the triangulation net as far as two kilometres toward the interior, for which we had to climb the big moraine. The optical telemeter by Goerz served us very well in establishing as exactly as possible equilateral triangles of four hundred metres in length. First, we marked the fifteen corners with bamboo poles that we stuck into the ice. But as soon as this was done, a foehn wind blew, accompanied by warm rain. Within a few days, thirty centimetres of the ice had melted and the poles loosened and toppled. I decided to replace them with numbered flat stones, as was done on the Rhone Glacier. A bamboo pole was planted only at set distances, this time three metres deep, so that the melting process could be measured.

These preparations, hampered by the inclement weather, took so much time that I started to worry whether we would ever manage to establish the seventeen points of the triangulation.

On 3 July, wonder of wonders, it stopped raining and there was no wind, and even better, the sun remained obscured too. No foehn and no sun – unbelievable luck. Only the mosquitoes were lurking. But we paid no attention to them, reached the base, and at 11 a.m. started the lengthy work of triangulation. I put the theodolite (a small Universal Hildebrandt, a fine instrument) into position and took aim. Jost walked unflaggingly with the regularity of an automaton and the patience of a border guard from one stone to the next, identifying it by lifting the measuring rod, and Stolberg, a man of unshakable composure, noted down the figures that I called out. What a joy to work with such assistants! We started on 3 July in the morning, and on the 4th at 4 a.m. we were still at work, determined to finish. When there were only four points left to locate, rain chased us away. We had not eaten since 5 p.m. the day before, and then only a few figs and some chocolate. A hearty soup would have improved the situation. We were happy to be able to finish the following night, but how tired we were!

On 6 July, we started on the southern outlet of the glacier. I planned to set two markers on its axis to observe simultaneously the movement and the retreat of the glacier. We reached it, with our instruments, through the gorge and the Kororsuak. There must have been a recent advance; all signs pointed to it. Now it seemed to be in retreat. The glacier splits up into several tongues. The ones on the right extend over a gentle slope; the tongue on the left falls partly into a narrow passage. The melt water flows through an impressive portal to the Eqip Kugsua. What a magnificent ice stream – like a mighty glacier in the Alps but without a moraine. We climbed onto it with rope and crampons, installed a marker pole in the lower pan, and then, over a large slope of firn snow, attained the rugged crevasses along the left-hand edge, and finally the middle of the glacier. The second marker we installed above the seracs. On our return, we crossed the glacier, which is quite fissured, then proceeded along the "Sunday Peak," and reached the station via the "Boulevard," as we called the path with the wonderful view.

Now, without any reservation, we could focus our energy on carrying out our pet project: to conquer the nunataks. Jost burned with impatience. Even if the risky undertaking were to fail, we would not have wasted our summer.

Our nunatak, about twenty-five kilometres north of the station, towered over a large ice plateau that slopes gently toward the nunatak near the Ilulialik. This slope appeared to be a continuation under the ice of the terrace on which our station stood. The eastern rim of this plateau is of equal average elevation and ends at the foot of a vast step, which rises to about eight hundred metres above the sea. The nunatak is rooted in this step, extending it toward the west in the form of a narrow ridge about three kilometres in length. The masses of ice dammed up by it curve sideways and split into two arms, which reunite further down in a wild confusion of seracs. The arm flowing on our side of the nunatak is roughly ten kilometres wide; in our direction, it borders on a less fissured strip, five kilometres wide, behind the Iiulialik nunatak. Two rows of fantastically formed white seracs close by contrast with the grey-yellow ice cap, showing that there are two more rapidly moving ice streams here. These are the ones that form the left-hand side of the Eqip Sermia. From where we stood, we estimated them to be around five kilometres wide. And this we would have to cross! Stolberg was dubious, shaking his head, as he already knew the Sennersuak (the great glacier, or ice sheet) and could tell stories about man-hauling sleds in the difficult Karajak area for 230 kilometres. We decided to go forward, for the time being, with one loaded sledge along the big moraine, despite the streams that crossed our path everywhere.

On a twenty-hour scouting march over numberless streams, we made it halfway to the nunatak. We found then what we had feared: the surface of the ice is completely broken up for three kilometres and even up to that point barely manageable for sledges. On the return trip, while trying to detour around the icy crevasses that were hindering our progress, we were caught in the network of watercourses that drain the whole area into an old lake. It took us an hour to extricate ourselves from the confusion of streams, which carved into the ice channels of up to eight metres wide and ten metres deep.

This reconnaissance, although discouraging in many ways, was successful in one point. Two-thirds of the way to the nunatak, we had spotted two dark specks that later proved to be moraines that we really had not expected at this point. From there, we planned to start our last and most difficult stretch to the nunatak.

Of course, we still had to leave the tent, the sled, all the heavy material, and unfortunately also the Primus stove five kilometres from the station. But I hoped that we could take enough food and instruments to the nunatak so that I could carry out my work.

We worked feverishly to prepare for the decisive march. Gaba and Immanuel helped to lug the needed material to the ice sheet. We packed our tent, Primus, theodolite, bamboo, and the sample pharmacy that Dr Cevey had given our group for the old sledge that had already seen action with de Quervain, Stolberg, and Baebler in 1909. In addition, all the backpacks had to come along, because there was so much to carry. Everything was securely tied down by Jost, who understands such things.

On 13 July, we made our departure at quarter to eleven in the evening.

My diary records the following remarks over the next days. Their brevity speaks volumes.

13 July. We are under way. The weather deteriorates; already light snow is falling, the sky is grey and overcast. Stolberg and I are hauling. Jost is steering from behind.

14 July. This has to be noted. The sledge overturned three times in a row; the third time the hoop at the front broke. Luckily, it is still usable. We each accept our roles, and we advance between endless streams without knocking into or blaming each other too much. A wet snow continues to fall, accompanied by fog. The temperature is 0°C and we are drenched in sweat. The snow sticks to the sledge runners. Two or three times we have fallen into iced-up cryoconite holes. By the time we reach our rest stop, I will be wet through, and so will Jost.

Toward 5 a.m., it is clearing. We go roughly in the right direction, but I cannot recognize the way we recently followed. But wait. Down to the left is a familiar glacier lake. We have to go back and detour around a crevasse-riddled hummock. The sledge speeds up. At the back Jost hangs on to it, but the sledge either overturns or skids into our ankles. We try to brake with all our might. Oh no! Another hump. And the fog and the crevasses start all over again. It is 7 o'clock. The weather is definitely bad. We camp. This is the western party's first bivouac on the ice. Soup, tea, and some sleep. We all feel cramps in our legs. Some clearing in the afternoon; the sun melts the new snow, the foehn starts up. At 2 p.m., we leave. We go downhill at giddy speed without getting stuck. Another run and we arrive at the rim of the first ice stream. This is where we leave the sledge and the heavy baggage.

15 July. Midnight. Laden with provisions, roped together and using crampons, we start toward one of those black specks on the ice, where we want to set up a cache. At first, we move too far west, into an impassable tangle of crevasses, and have to retrace our steps almost as far as the sledge. But then we manage to get across the first ice stream, reaching the "plain" that separates us from the second one.

We cross this place without too many difficulties, despite deep ice gorges that we shall have a chance to get to know more thoroughly later. We traverse the plain with the above-mentioned ominous lake, and from there it is uphill again. Then, suddenly, around a bend, the moraine comes into sight. Impressive! We reach it at half past eight. The foehn is blowing violently and, since 4 p.m., the sky has been overcast again.

We set up a food cache at the top end of the moraine. We are tired and hungry. Behind a knoll, we find some cover from the strong wind. We sleep for a long time in our *timiaks*;[4] then we warm some milk in Stolberg's little saucepan and eat the biscuits I received from a kind sister.

After having set up this food cache as an indispensable support base on the moraine, we have to go back to fetch the instruments before we advance further toward the nunatak. At 2:30, we depart on the rope and against the wind, which drives the rain into our faces. Jost is leading with astonishing confidence. We are going well, but the sledge is still far away. We are tired. Here we are at the second ice stream, which we have to climb. We happen to go a little too far east and find ourselves in a system of astonishingly deep crevasses. We have to move along vertiginous ridges, endlessly hacking out steps, upward and down. Jost up front has a very secure footing and a practised eye, keeping unfailingly to our course. We others feel our exhaustion and admire his mastery. He revels in the fullness of his strength.

Finally, we reach the plateau again and see the lake in the distance. The rain has stopped but there is fog in the air. What on earth would we have done in this fog yesterday?

On the second glacier stream, we get into an area of crevasses – enormous, magnificent crevasses. But we have had enough. Jost has to turn back. Another detour, but soon we reach the sledge. We set up the tent. All three of us are exhausted and enervated. A strong soup and a good sleep will improve everything. We have made two marches for eight and a half hours, strenuously, with only one hour of rest each time!

The rain started again and with it a howling southwestern wind. The ice is deteriorating surprisingly fast; in vain, we try to anchor the tent with our ice pick.

16 July: A dreadful night and an equally dreadful day. The wind shook our overly light tent furiously. Totally soaked by the driving rain, it is dripping all

---

4 "In South Greenland the men wear upon their body what is called a timiak. It is made of bird-skins, with the feathers or down turned inwards, is shaped very much like our woolen jerseys, and, like them, is drawn over the head. The timiak is provided with a hood, used as a head-covering in the open air; at other times it is thrown back, and forms, with its upstanding selvage of black dog-skin, a sort of collar round the neck" (Fridtjof Nansen, *Eskimo Life* [London: Longmans Green, 1893]).

over. Jost, on the other hand, who is not lying near the dripping walls, has his feet in a lake that he is bailing out with his cup. The icy floor is our least of our worries; the rain running down the walls is digging a safety trench all around us. But the ceiling! *Ajorpok, agsut Aajorpadlakaok*! (It goes badly, it goes extremely badly, very much!) Little by little, the water penetrates everywhere; without our timiaks, which we luckily we brought back from the moraine and without our porous waterproofs, which do as well as they can, it would be a disaster. Stolberg is worst off. His sleeping bag, an old companion, is made of separate pieces sewn together. The poor man's teeth are chattering; for a time, I fear for his health.

Finally, the wind abates, but it rains all the harder. This time I am bailing, or better if I don't bail. It doesn't help anyway. Rolled up in my sleeping bag, I don't stir and feel reasonably warm. My diary I keep on my chest to keep it from getting soaked. We sleep hardly at all and make vociferous complaints. Jost and I philosophically smoke our pipes, and sometimes we have a discussion.

Stolberg lets me know that he intends to let us go alone to the nunatak. Our "senior" feels that he is no longer up to the storms, and he fears he would be a hindrance where we have to make dangerous jumps over crevasses that cannot be detoured. I understand and agree, although his strong shoulders would have been most welcome to carry loads. But he has lived through a lot of bold adventures in the past.

The two of us will us go alone. But the theodolite and the camera have to come along at all cost. We are not here for sport. Stolberg will return to the station and then come to meet us in a week's time.

17 July: The rain has finally stopped. The sun looks pale, but it warms the tent and the tent hooks that came loose in the rain hold again. The cryoconite holes, which had shrunk by at least thirty centimetres, grow deeper again. We organize a big dry-out. We really don't want to carry water with us. The mood improves. An asparagus soup, a surprise from Stolberg, helps too.

At 5 p.m. our friend Stolberg leaves, and at 9 p.m. we too start off, each carrying twenty-five kilograms or more on our backs. Besides the theodolite, the tripod, and the camera, there are other indispensable items; on top of all, our sleeping bags bob back and forth. The only provision we take is some chocolate, since there is more than enough food in our cache on the moraine. Despite the heavy loads, we make good progress, this time going along the lake and then keeping at the height of the plateau, in order to shorten, if possible, the distance over the second ice stream. Vain hope! Long crevasses and then actual chasms bar our passage.

18 July: It takes us three and a half hours just to get to the ice stream, and four hours more to traverse it. We have to jump over clefts that yawn appallingly.

I admire Jost's secure footing. Once he has to step onto an ice bridge that bridges a massive crevasse. The ledge is so narrow that Jost has to stand sideways, feet close together, to hack steps with his ice pick from the side. I am standing farther down and can see clearly that he is trembling from the effort, and that our rope is stretched to its limits. The rising ledge is twenty-five metres long. Once on top, he can find solid footing again, and I can move up, too. I measure the blue depths with a glance – nobody can be permitted to fall here – and then I am across, but this was very off-putting. Similar "exercises" are repeated often, although none are as risky.

We have arrived at the second "plain." We walk side by side, talking. Already we see the moraine. There will be food, and then we can sleep. It is 8:30 and we are very close to the moraine. But what a strange sight! It is dreadfully high. And where we had to climb down eight metres to the base, we now walk horizontally. And what is this blue ice wall at the end of this yawning canyon? And this pond? We put down our baggage and check. With difficulty, I climb the moraine, the ground giving way under every step. No trace of the cache! To the east a lake, a deep canyon, numerous streams, and further up more seracs.

This cannot be our moraine; it has to lie more to the east, and we must have missed it. But how could that be? We take our packs up again, climb on, wade through streams, and complain angrily. But, even from above, we find nothing. Full of doubt, we wonder whether we really did go far enough to the northeast. Again, we put down our packs and go in different directions to search.

Soon Jost returns with a gloomy expression. "Found nothing!"

"Me neither!"

We stare at each other. Suddenly, we are struck by a clear and horrifying revelation: this *is* our moraine, but the cache isn't there any longer. A lake has drained through the puzzling new canyon, carrying with it everything, and totally reshaping the moraine. Not a trace of the marker bamboo or of our provisions. In one fell swoop, we have lost all the support for our work. And the nunatak is there, so very close. What a bitter disappointment!

Should we leave our heavy baggage and go back to the station for fresh provisions? But the way back is so long and dangerous. And where would our stuff really be safe? What if the bad weather returns? We are so hungry and exhausted; above all, we have to sleep. Where we are now, we would not be able to withstand an icy southeasterly wind. We pull what is necessary from our bags and walk back toward the moraine. Jost, tricked by his glasses, walks directly toward a trench with a wild stream. A shout, and he is in the water. I jump on top of the rope, but he is already climbing out of the water. His crampons have saved his life. A few metres farther down, the water falls into a deep cauldron.

He has lost his ice axe but has managed to keep his timiak and sleeping bag, which is now soaked. There is no way we can go on. So we stay in this ravine, exposed to the north wind, but in the sun. It is 10:30 a.m. Jost strips off, shivering in the cold. I try in vain to fish his ice axe out of the raging water. Then I stand in the wind to shelter him. Then we rant and fume about our porous waterproofs until their reputation is totally shredded. Cold, we crawl into them, without being able to get a wink of sleep. Wind and melt water penetrate.

At 2:30 in the afternoon, disabled, we get ready to turn back. Jost has no food left; I still have three sticks of meat-chocolate left. Two of them we save till we reach the second ice stream, the third one we share. We dry our equipment in the raw southeasterly wind. In the meantime, we want to photograph the moraine. Perhaps we can find some vestiges of our cache. Nothing! We have lost eighteen pieces of pemmican, six bars of chocolate, a tin of Zwieback, five tins of butter, a similar amount of milk, two tins of jam, a nice piece of ham, soups, tea, sugar, all our figs, a third of Jost's marvellous honey, homemade biscuits, the bamboo poles and Stolberg's cooker. If the weather had not been so bad the day before yesterday, our timiaks would have been included.

It is 6 p.m. With heavy hearts, we pick up our baggage and start our retreat. At the beginning, it works fine, but my vision in my right eye is disturbed. I see everything double. Does that come from hunger?

Slowly we approach the second ice stream, with a rest stop every hour. We are too distressed even to talk. From here on, it will be difficult. We have subdued our stomachs with our last chocolate.

Here are the crevasses, the twenty-metre deep ones, fifty metres wide and hundred metre long ones, the ledges, and the old snow bridges. We walk safely, but this time there are many stops. It is difficult to keep our packs from throwing us off balance. The hours pass, and there still are towering ice walls, again new gorges open up. The traverse lasts from 10:30 in the evening until three in the morning of 19 July. At each rest stop, I am overcome by almost inexorable sleep. Thirst is racking us. Jost never loses his guiding instinct; carefully but decisively, he hacks steps, detours, or jumps over crevasses. What an alpinist!

Finally, the lake comes into view, the terrain improves. But our shoulders hurt, and we have the wind tugging at our packs. We take off the rope to walk more freely. Every fifteen minutes we rest, and so we finally reach the sled. We have been under way for thirty-four hours.

We refresh ourselves on the tins of condensed milk. Suddenly I feel a very sharp pain in my left eye. I have an eye inflammation, so painful that I can't keep my eyes open any longer to help Jost to set up the tent in the strong winds.

We stay here for two days. On 21 July, in a dreadful foehn storm, we arrive back at the station. Stolberg welcomes us with open arms. The wind, which blows at eighteen metres a second, keeps us from setting up the tent we brought along. So we sleep in the storage tent among all the instruments. Later we found a wide array of items blown into the rocks, even big square metal tins.

On 31 July, we leave the station. Autumn has come, and our work here is finished. With the help of old Christensen and porters from Ata, we transport everything in one night down to Quervainshavn.

On 1 August, they take me in their beautiful light-blue umiak to Ata, where I am received with unexpected honours (the prophet abroad!), a gunshot salute, and the Danish flag hoisted aloft. I answer with the small Swiss flag that I took out of the case that my admired friend F.A. Forel had given me for the 1 August celebration. Is this reception possibly linked by telepathy to a similar one that is accorded at the same time to our expedition leader at Angmagssalik? At any rate, Pavia Jensen, the excellent Greenlander and chief of Ata, overwhelms me with kindness and good things. For breakfast, he serves butter and jam made from Greenlandic blueberries, and for lunch, baked seal, which tastes delicious.

Bright sunshine glitters on the quiet fjord and on the huge icebergs, the same sunshine that shines on the faraway blue mountains of our home for the celebration of 1 August. When I leave, Mrs Pavia, who remarks my taste for her baking, gives me a fresh loaf of bread, and for Stolberg I take cigars. For weeks he has had a hankering for them.

But we could celebrate our national holiday at Quervainshavn only on 4 August, a Sunday, our first free day since Holstensborg. We shoot some gulls in the nearby rocks. Our tent is comfortably decorated, on a moss ledge, two steps from the sea, in the shadow of a rock massif, next door to the depot and opposite the glacier. Here we pass the most agreeable days of the summer, as long as it is not raining. But, sad to say, the rain starts again on 6 August and continues for five days and five nights. I worry about the triangulation on the inland ice sheet, which we will have to repeat one more time, if we want to know the movement of the ice in the intervening time. What if the snow covers up our marker stones? Time passes quickly.

On 10 August, the weather clears. Loaded like beasts of burden, we return with Immanuel for a last time to the station at the ice sheet. For the last time, we find shelter in the Greenland tent, which we have to put up again and again after storms blow it down.

And now the game starts again. I am behind the theodolite, Stolberg takes notes, and Jost walks with the rod from stone to stone. No sooner have we finished than the snow covers everything. Our station, which looked so pretty in summer, now offers a melancholy picture. All the little flowers have faded long ago.

The observations at the southern glacier have to be repeated as well. These are made amidst snow showers. Finally, better weather lets us undertake the photogrammetry of the glacier. In the evening, at 9:30, we descend for the last time from the inland ice sheet to the ocean. The summer's work is complete.

There is still some secondary work, some happy hunting. And then the whaling boat of the minister from Jakobshavn and the umiak from Ata arrive to pick us up. Jost and Stolberg, who are looking forward to their stay on Disko, are less downcast than myself, who will be mired deep in the hurly-burly of European affairs within a few weeks. We were so comfortable here without politics, collars, ties, and newspapers.

On 19 August in the evening, we finish packing. This is difficult, because the young people of the eastern party, in their hurry, have managed to manhandle the lids of the boxes, despite all our fatherly advice, and the Greenlanders have used them as firewood.

We depart. The invincible armada is made up of the whaler which is towing the *Ella* fixed up à la diable and lightly loaded. On the masthead flutters the Swiss flag, and at the stern sits a Greenlander, bailer in hand. Then follows the umiak, ably steered by Immanuel. It tows the kayaks. Gaba, as auxiliary cruiser, but unarmed, manoeuvres alongside between the icebergs, checks on seals, and retrieves the gulls we shoot with our last ammunition.

The glacier appears in its entire magnificence. Fall has modified its blue tones: in the dusk of the coming polar night, it looks almost greyish. The Sermerk Kangidlemek appears only as a fine white line in the distance.

In order to warm up, I slip into my kayak, and then we continue, Gaba and I, on the open sea, past icebergs, in the semi-darkness for nineteen kilometres without halt. At 2 a.m., we land at Ata. Gaba, proud of his pupil, wakes the colony with a rifle shot. Pavia and his wife come down, bringing warm coffee and buttered bread. Ajungipadlakaok! Very good indeed! One hour later the "fleet" arrives too, and the welcome starts all over again.

We camp in the "village square." The men of Ata accept with pleasure the spoils of the expedition: rye bread, metal tins. Above all, our bamboo wands are highly prized. In the end, Pavia organizes a Greenlandic ball with refreshments in our honour. Gaba puts on his catechist's vestment and dances like a dervish. At the end, we have a concert: Swiss yodellers and psalm-singing by the locals.

Next morning we leave, Gaba and I, in our kayaks along the western shore of Ata Sound. This was a good choice: as soon as we are opposite the mouth of the

Kangerdluarsuk Fjord, we dance on the waves like corks, although, strangely, we at first don't feel the foehn wind that creates the waves. But we do meet it when the umiak, which we are escorting, heads toward the eastern shore. Gaba and I, the spray flying around our ears, fight the storm and paddle in competition with the bigger boat. "Agsut" (it goes badly), shouts the laughing crew, and *Agsut* has remained the name of my precious craft.

Soon we are in the shadow of the big rock at Kitsenniut for the last bivouac of our nomadic life. Late at night, I'm still listening to the Greenlanders' melancholy singing.

I feel the twenty-five kilometres of the stormy fjord in my arms. Next day we sail with a favourable wind toward Rodebay. Niels Robsch, a Greenlander, receives us at his place. He is sixty-eight years old, and he tells us with pride that in spring he was still able to catch eight *kailaluit* (white whales).

Gaba and I reach Jakobshavn on 22 August, again by kayak. This time we lag far behind the umiak, which is steered by Pavia. And like some Viking of old, blond-bearded Jost sits enthroned behind the square sail of the antique vessel.

In Jakobshavn, Jost is billeted at the pastor's, Stolberg and I at commercial assistant Krogh's. Although he is just about to move, he offers us his unstinted hospitality.

The blue umiak has already left. It hurts to see the small silhouette of Gaba, our friendly, intelligent companion, fade away, together with those of Immanuel and Pavia. I had time enough for one last visit to Jakobshavn Fjord, now completely filled with ice.

On 28 August, to the astonishment of the Danes, I board the *storboot*, the little sailboat that plies Disko Bay if the wind is favourable, alone with my baggage. In Godhavn, I shall have to wait for the *Hans Egede*, which will take me to Europe.

Again, gun salutes, hat-waving, and parting farewell wishes. I see the somewhat melancholy faces of my friends grow smaller and smaller. For a long time, they watch the Swiss flag, which is now homeward bound, leaving them there for the long winter. Then they turn toward their new future. My feelings of friendship and my thanks for all their help remain with them.

Forty-eight hours at sea seem short with all the entertainment that the sea offers. At any moment, big seals can lift their remarkable heads out of the water. A magnificent whale appears and, in one mighty breath, blows a cloud of vapour into the air.

In Godhavn, at the Danish-Arctic Station, I am the guest of our friend Magister Porsild, who is also expecting Stolberg and Jost.

How I would like to stay here. Fortunately, the *Hans Egede* is delayed. I still have time to repeat the measurements of Frode Petersen in Blasedal and to verify the glacier's retreat.

On 6 September, the *Hans Egede*, although overbooked, takes me on board with official permission. In Godthaab, I go on land a final time to see Ny Herrnhut, with its little old huts. A solitary, very old woman crouches beside the empty fireplace and smokes a cracked porcelain pipe in view of the ocean, which she can hardly see, for she is half blind. An emblem of human frailty and the vanity of human striving in the face of unchanging eternity!

In the morning, when we sail out to sea, I again see the miserable hut of old Kaladlit disappear, a small fleck, while the proud facade of the Godthaab seminary stands clear in front of a green background. The young civilization of the Greenlanders pushes aside the old and dying Eskimo culture.

On deck, an elderly Danish couple stand by themselves and quietly watch the land disappear. They have given so many years of their lives to this country, which in all probability they will never see again. And I feel the same, although I was here only a few months. Yet I love this country like a second home.

A WINTER IN GREENLAND

AUGUST STOLBERG

Summer guests are no longer so rare on the west coast of Greenland, but when the midnight dusk deepens as the sun sinks into polar night and the sparse tussocks of plant life take on a prematurely withered hue, these men of science follow the daylight southward. Thus our Professor Mercanton left us on 28 August in Jakobshavn. On the last boat sailing to Europe, the barque *Thorvaldsen*, Dr Jost and I sailed south for a short distance to Egedesminde. There the leader of the Danish-Arctic Station on Disko, Magister Porsild, picked us up in his motor launch, *Clio borealis*. We were the first winter guests at the station since its inception, the first willing to test Porsild's dictum that a winter spent in the Arctic was an Elysium for any scholar.

As soon as we crossed over to Godhavn, we started taking the imminent Arctic winter into account by stopping at the "dog island" – *nomen est omen* – and acquiring six wonderfully strong near-white dogs to make up a team for Jost. As the sea had turned unfriendly and would not allow us to travel onwards, we stayed overnight with the dog islanders. The dark evening was used to covertly dig up a cranium from an old rock tomb for anthropological studies. And we enjoyed a little dance party. The next day it was 5 p.m. before we dared to board the *Clio* again. A very strong phosphorescence accompanied us during the voyage. The fragments of drift ice shone with a mysterious luminescence. Luckily, we did not hit any of them.

On the way, we also had to set down the young midwife of Kronprinsens Island at her station. This island lady is so courageous that she will travel in a kayak to bring help as quickly as possible in an emergency. No young hunter has managed yet to tie this Amazon to his hearth. On Disko Bay, her married colleague Susanna is no less determined a woman, as we were later to learn.

Once, without any outside help, she had to amputate one of her own fingers using an ordinary pair of scissors and a knife after she suffered blood poisoning in the course of her duties.

On 16 September, we arrived at the Danish Arctic Station in Godhavn. An introduction to this unique scientific institute, which would host us for the winter, may be of some interest to the reader. The station is situated a kilometre to the northeast of the large settlement of Godhavn, at roughly 70° north. It was established in the autumn of 1909 and the following winter according to the plans of Magister Porsild. The initiative came from Porsild, who was able to mobilize private donors in Copenhagen, while the Danish government has so far provided operational subsidies that are unfortunately only temporary.

The station has a dual role. First, its principal, Magister Porsild himself, works on scientific questions of the Arctic, predominantly in biology and ethnography but also in the geophysical realm. Second, it is intended to serve as a round-the-year base for Danish and foreign researchers. Hitherto, the latter kind had not made use of this valuable opportunity to overwinter here. The few summer months are insufficient to complete research on some questions. For embryologists, for instance, the winter hunting season brings in the best specimens.

Built entirely of wood, the station comprises a residence with a laboratory. There is room for two visiting scientists to stay. There is also an apartment for helpers, a workshop, a storage shed, a seismological and an astronomical hut, and a heated chicken coop. Rounding out the facilities are the above-mentioned motor launch and several sailing and rowing boats. We thus found at the station many resources that we would otherwise have had to acquire for ourselves at extra cost. Considering the difficult requirements for such an institute and the unfavourable external conditions, one can appreciate the very special abilities demanded from its principal. The scholarly magister, beside his scientific work, is capable equally of mending a watch or building a sledge with metal runners. He is scientist, carpenter, instrument-maker, and blacksmith all in one. He also has medical knowledge, which is particularly important as there is no other healer on the whole island and often a waiting time of three-quarters of a year between visits by the doctor from Jakobshavn. Magister Porsild is the right man in the right place. His wife and three children live with him at the station.

From the station, one has an unlimited view of the sea. The area forms a kind of bridge between the round hills of gneiss and the basalt landscape. Between the station and the sea there is a lagoon of brackish water that remains frozen for at least nine months of the year. Further out toward the sea is a flat strip of black basaltic sand one kilometre long. Here Magister Porsild set up a wooden working hut for us. This then was the locus where in the winter of 1912–13 we were to sacrifice hecatombs of pilot balloons, kites, and captive balloons in the service of aerology, often with whitened noses and tear-filled eyes.

In the days after our arrival, the southwesterly that we had feared on Dog Island blew up and raged out in the Davis Strait. This time we received only its enormous swells. It was astonishingly quiet, except for the roar of the breakers. This is often observed in storms from the southwest, but there is no explanation. It is possible that the wind is deflected by the high basalt walls. Their effects were frequently a nuisance when we were launching kites.

In the fall, a sudden squall once carried one of our instrumented kites out to sea. An iceberg was kind enough to snag the cable, and so the instrument could be recovered by boat in the nick of time. It was certainly not always pleasant to work outside, but we took advantage of every suitable hour. So we passed our days in alternating practical work outside and doing theoretical evaluation indoors at the station. In December, we made two attempts at lofting our instruments on pilot balloons, but the polar night was too far advanced; we had to cancel this part of our program until the end of January in order not to waste our equipment. The pilot balloons were tracked according to the method developed by Dr de Quervain. Thanks to the clear atmosphere in high northern latitudes, the wind conditions that are so important to the question of the air circulation in the Arctic and of the existence of a related polar cyclone could be observed often to the limit of the troposphere, and in a few cases even far beyond. Our pilot balloon no. 98 was observed to 16,400 metres above sea level, no. 99 to 22,400 metres, and no. 92 probably went as far as the immense altitude of 39,000 metres.

At the beginning of October, animal life was still quite active along the shore. Uncounted gulls and ravens shared with the dogs the rich pickings offered by the sea. Huge quantities of little crabs and thousands of small cod – already more or less frozen – lay around. After a while, the dogs' jaws tired of them, and they ate no more. A Greenlander dog and satiation are usually a contradiction in terms. If enough food is offered, the sledge dog will eat until he is ready to burst. Indeed, he may burst, as Amundsen has testified. The Greenlanders themselves do not eat this cod. Thorbjorn Porsild, however, found a remarkable use for them. When the frame of our work hut was completed, he hung, instead of the usual wreath of flowers, a wreath of these small fish.

The coming of winter was already quite obvious. On 7 October, sailing to the innermost corner of the Disko Fjord where Porsild has a cabin, we encountered so much ice that *Clio* with her thin planks had to give up her attempts to cut through. By mid-October, we could walk across the Rödelf, and the children were skating on the puddles. Our work was progressing well; the daylight faded more and more as the northern lights increased. But anybody who imagines that the desire to sleep increases with diminishing daylight and that in midwinter the people in Greenland hold veritable sleep orgies is very wrong. As far as bedtime was concerned, we might have been living in a big city. What with telling stories, reading, playing cards, even sleigh-riding and walking in the moonlight, and, last but not least, drinking coffee, we usually stayed up till 2 a.m. and sometimes even longer. As we had to take the first measurements at 8 a.m. and breakfast was served at 9 a.m., our night's rest was of short duration, as Dr Jost in particular can testify.

Really, drinking coffee and smoking in Greenland! These narcotics are prized by Europeans and natives alike. "This is our only solace," Mrs Porsild once said of coffee. Concerning pipes and their smoke clouds, I quietly suspect that the frequent and so troublesome fogs in the Davis Strait may not be a manifestation of condensation alone.

After a monumental struggle lasting for months, the sea finally succumbs to the cold. Even into January, some areas adjacent to the shore remained open, pond-like, similar to breathing holes in the ocean. Here the surf was still pounding. Ice plates move back and forth in the strong movement, the larger fragments rising and falling in the rhythm of the waves without losing their station. As if seeking a way out of a cage, everything undulates heavily, until the mushy mass finally forms one solid cover. Like a vanquished animal, the surf growls less and less in front of the Rödelf's mouth. The icebergs near the shore are now walled in by the ice, and to the south certain blank patches show that the frost has started its work of crystallization. The sea is dying.

And before this, the daylight had died, too! Early in November, the sun lifts itself only a few degrees above the horizon. Dawn and sunset glow together. At noon, the evening sunlight fills my room, which looks south. The southern horizon presents a beautiful sight. Iceberg cities with gates, towers, and battlements contrast sharply with the golden foil that frames the slate-grey sea and the clouds. By the end of November, during vigorous snowstorms, the fiery eye of the stove and the lamp burned all day long.

The Rödelf had been safe for sledging for a long while. We often drove between its canyon walls, which were partly clad in soft green ice, as far as the cirque where frozen waterfalls closed off the stark scene. On 28 November, on a drive above the waterfalls on the mirror-smooth arms of the river in the Blase Valley, the reflected sun appeared shortly before noon, barely above the horizon. A solemn solitude, an icy stillness, surrounded us between the white table mountains. The sky in the south took on an apple-green tint with orange-yellow accents, while the northern sky in the shadow of the earth turned a blackish blue. With this beautiful picture, the sun took its leave for seven weeks.

The highest praise in the Arctic winter, however, should go to the sledge dog. Only dog-sleds would let us take shorter or longer trips and to gain a special experience of nature. A man without a sledge and a team is like a cripple. But you need not only dogs but also "dog sense." This knowledge has its ultimate expression in the mastery of the whip. It was quite an accomplishment that Jost managed to weld the untrained dogs that we had bought on Dog Island into a good team of sled-haulers, and this in a relatively short time. I was present several times at the initial training, acting as a sandbag on the sled. This happened early in fall, when there were many stretches without snow. Thus the wild ride went cross-country, up the terraces and down again. Above all, down! That was great fun. I was astonished that a Greenland sled, even one made by Porsild himself, could withstand such jolting and jumping. After one such dog trip, a particularly rough one that cost two whips, Jost told me, "You did your job as well as the dogs. That was a nasty ride." Yes, indeed. But these all-but-wild untrained dogs were later to heed their master almost to the letter.

As Christmas drew closer, a "Christmas tree" started to grow in the workshop, a wooden scaffolding that was painted brown and then arrayed with cranberry twigs. Once adorned with the usual Christmas decorations, it looked much more life-like than expected. However, it lacked the exquisite smell of pine. But what else could one do? Once, the Magister had received a real Christmas tree from Denmark on the last voyage of the *Hans Egede*. But this won no favour from the children, Thorbjörn, Erling, and little Asta. That was no Christmas tree, he was told; next time they would prefer to have a "real" one again!

In Greenland, the shortest day, 21 December, is considered a sort of a preliminary holiday. To celebrate, there was a torte in the evening, but at 1 a.m. Porsild declared, "We should do something tonight." So we drove in several sleighs along the Rödelf up to the cirque. The ice was like a mirror, and the sleighs skidded quite a bit. It was unbelievably quiet, and the moon shone so brightly that one could have read outside. Soon we were at the frozen waterfall, which was still murmuring beneath its mask of ice. The surrounding walls were clad in ice, with steep black and brown rakes in between. Much of the snow had been blown in from the side into the sheltered hollow of the canyon. A blue-black sky arched over everything, and down from a rock sounded Jost's beautiful baritone voice. Soon the dogs had raced us back to the station, where a breakfast prepared by the admirable Mrs Porsild ended the day.

Then on 24 December arrived the "dejlige Jul." Many a greasy note of paper money was exchanged by the Greenlanders for coffee at the store. No celebration could take place without a sufficient supply of this miraculous beverage in the hut! Just as in Switzerland, a parcel-carrying figure approached the station in the twilight of the 24th. This figure was old Leonore, who back in 1909 had helped de Quervain, Baebler, and myself with housekeeping. Leonore's parcel was for me! It contained a pair of kamiks, which I could put to good use. Some kroner notes and a colourful ribbon were ready for the bearer of gifts. She expressed her pleasure over the unexpected reciprocal gift as follows: "My mind is shaking in my head." And with shaking mind, she hurried back to the colony as quickly as she could to tell of her good fortune.

In the afternoon, the whole station rushed on sleighs to the colony to the nicely illuminated but overcrowded little church, not much bigger than a large room. A "tree" was lit, and Pastor Mortensen, a giant of a man, led the service. The mass of people, the candles, the lit tree, and the well-stoked stove increased the temperature in the crowded church to a point that not all of the Europeans present could withstand. The minister read the gospel of Christmas in Greenlandic and Danish. Then they sang "Silent Night, Holy Night" in Greenlandic, the beloved old melody sounding out as beautifully as at home. Our catechist Kleist must have liked this refrain particularly well, for he also played it on the venerable harmonium at other seasons, at weddings, christenings, and any other suitable occasion.

In the course of the evening, we exchanged gifts at the station. Earlier the Greenlanders came and sang hymns while the snowflakes floated down more and more thickly through the pitch-black night. According to Danish custom, we held hands and sang "Gläde Jul, dejlige Jul, Engle dale ned i Skjul," as we circled around the tree. The gifts were brought by a "Cape Yorker" who had just arrived on his sledge via Upernavik. I may reveal that the fur-clad man was Thorbjörn Porsild himself.

On the second day in the afternoon, Jost and I had a visit from the catechist and six other Greenlanders, including some hunters. They admired our European weapons and mountain boots, and Jost had to sing. Several small glasses of *snapsemik* and many cigars brought life and a pleasant atmosphere to the room. The stove added its contribution, and so did the lamps and a miniature private Christmas tree from the Vosges Mountains, until the temperature in the room finally reached the level that Greenlanders require to get into a really festive mood. The airing of the room could not take place until 9 April, as my storm windows were kept nailed shut (for 168 days).

The following day was a day of tests for Jost and myself. We had to thank in person each of our guests for yesterday's visits and to make a visit ourselves, or *polarpok* as the Greenlanders say. This *polarpoken* isn't so easy, as one has to accept coffee everywhere and take a drink too.

"Invigorated" by about twenty cups of coffee, we two *angalassoks* – vagabonds, as we are known officially among the natives – returned tested and fully accepted to the station. Of course, right away they offered us the same drink. The offer came from Magister Porsild. Following precedent, we were in the mood "to kill him dead then and there," but changed our mind as this universally gifted man would probably soon be needed again to repair some instrument for us. Our forbearance was actually rewarded in much the same vein later. On 29 December, the Christmas season ended with a distribution of sweets, toy pistols, coloured pencils, flutes (!), and so on to the colony's children by Pastor Mortensen and his wife in the little church. And thus the eventful year that had passed so quickly came to an end with songs and fireworks in front of the station.

Snow and ice had made an excellent road to the colony, and we often sped back and forth with the dogs. In summer, however, the tides created a six- to seven-metre-wide trench right in front of the colony, which was difficult to cross. It was therefore not an unreasonable idea to collect the losses from card games in order to finance a bridge at this spot. Even so, gambling is a vice and rightly punished, as experienced by two young gentlemen from our station, the assistant Richard Jensen and the private teacher Moller-Pedersen. They had driven up for a game of "L'Hombre" at the colony. As usual, the dogs remained outside in their harnesses. By the time the card play was over, the dogs had finished eating up their traces, and so the drivers had to wander on foot back to the station through the deep snow.

Winter allows time to dream. We preferred to recall the events of the summer and imagined the eastern party fighting barbaric inland ice tribes. It was Mercanton's fault that I once disturbed the night rest of the whole station. I had dreamed that his piccolo flute, which he had brought with him on the *Hans Egede* and even onto the ice cap for his own pleasure, had grown long legs and was trampling me pitilessly in polka measure!

After the little sleigh rides on land, which I have already mentioned, there came the time in January when the sea also turned into a long-awaited road for sledges. At the beginning of the year, however, it was not quite frozen enough. In the bay near the colony, there was only thin ice, often moving like a carpet of cloth. The dogs would walk on it, but humans had to take great care. Some hunters dared to advance to the edge of the ice, carrying their kayaks on their heads, and probing with a stick, to catch seals or even narwhales or white whales. When such a man comes up on the skyline, one sees at first only the front of the kayak bobbing with each step. It does not take much imagination to see a dinosaur loping along in some primeval era. The monster turns out to be a Greenlander dragging a killed seal behind him. Eagerly, the dogs eye the animal and sniff the traces of blood on the wide track, which wildly excites their appetites.

On 13 January, the station took three sledges on a short tour over the frozen sea. It was easy to avoid some spots of unsafe ice. At first, it was a somewhat strange sensation for me to leave solid land behind, to see the shore recede, and to flit along on a sledge where the breakers used to be and where the deep dark sea lurked beneath. Once, a stretch of ice perhaps one night old moved like a heavy carpet under the sled, but otherwise the condition of the ice was good. We drove along the Skarvefjeld. Since this ride along the Skarvefjeld is probably the most magnificent scenic experience offered by the entire shoreline of Disko Bay, we should, I think, allow ourselves to add a more extensive description. Jost writes the following:

> Even though the Disko Mountains, in places over a thousand metres high, appear from far away as if cut from a stack of boards with saw and straight-edge, because the layers of basalt and volcanic stuff are hardly disturbed and are visible from far away, some parts offer a most impressive sight when viewed from close up. In particular, the Skarvefjeld east of Godhavn rises like an enormous bastion vertically out of the briny waters with rock walls a hundred metres and higher, and towers and pinnacles. Where the powers of nature had carved deep clefts into this rampart, one beholds high up the sharp forms of the mountain summits towering like gothic cathedrals above all else, backed by a sky that is almost cobalt blue. The overall impression is magnificent, but the detailed forms are varied. There are secret bays and grottos and enormous caves, elephants' heads with trunks tucked into the mountain, soaring arches reflected in the waters. At times, their surfaces are irregularly stippled, or they may spring up from delicate columns, as if skilfully crafted by a stonemason. Then there are the huge black pillars washed by the waves, standing guard at a slight distance from the gigantic castle. Every form that the keenest fantasy could imagine is reality here. This is, in short, a theatrical backdrop of extraordinary enchantment.

Let it remain undecided whether it is the view in summer with the open sea, or in winter with snow and ice, that is the more impressive. The colour effects may be more powerful in winter when the snow is blowing from the terraces. At that time, perhaps, the language of fairy tales makes itself more clearly heard. Where the shore curves inward and forms a single headwater, at Kwinek (the place where the angelica grows), there hangs in winter icy stalactite on pale-green stalactite, like tiers of drapery, each high as a house. The falling waters ceaselessly shape the ice, forming corners, niches, grottos, and passages. A secret creativity is at work here, one that is unknown to summer. Despite the icy surroundings, unseen warm springs murmur in secret. Other bays are surrounded by high walls. As the snow does not lodge on them, it leaves these walls a dun colour but drifts into great rolls above their crests. Above this the vast massif, more than a thousand metres high, takes on a pale red tone when the midwinter sun hovers a bare few minutes above the horizon. When the sun shines again in spring, these fronts are sharply lit in lively yet harmonious hues between the white landscape of the sea and the blue sky. Silver-grey, sulphur-coloured, dark ochre, and brown in every shade between, they stand in contrast with the snow on their peaks.

When the sun is covered and the fjeld is wrapped in fog, revealing only a scattering of its summits, and rocks sheared off by the frost rattle invisibly down, one's thoughts roam ahead to a fog-shrouded future era. When all love and desire and, with it, all creation in this human world is extinguished, these mountain altars will stare into space like a monument to the life-sustaining planet. Already they are posting a warning signal. Born in fire, they belong to a period when the earth was young and strong, long ago.

To the south extends the loneliness of the frozen sea. Groups of icebergs here and there interrupt the almost limitless horizon line. Sometimes, sledge tracks meander between them. Farther out, silvery glints betray the open sea. The sky stretches its pallid azure over this enormous plain and, between the veil of cirrus and cumulus clouds, the spring sun gleams. I went on a dozen drives under the Skarvefjeld in summer and winter. For those who overwinter at Disko, this is the reward. It is quite impossible to capture these theatrical and romantic scenes with the camera. When will a painter arrive here who can represent this world? When you have good ice conditions and cold, still weather at the same time, travelling by dog sledge is unrivalled. The subdued crunching of the sledge runners and the soft sound of the whip's trailing thong can almost lull you to sleep when you are comfortably installed on your sledge, half-sitting, half-lying. However, it is impossible to make any binding contract with the powers that pull us, and the dogs knot up their traces in no time. Even well-trained dogs are no docile lambs in the long run. Snappish as they are, they keep the peace among themselves only for an interval, and the fights that break out periodically lead to a tangle of traces. That's when even a phlegmatic driver gets to be temperamental, a European even more so than a Greenlander. The European loses the varnish of civility. He swears loudly, and so does the Greenlander, the latter, however, in his more moderate way. He speaks to the dogs thus: "Look at you, and you call yourself a dog? He isn't a dog at all, he is a codfish. Yes, a codfish is what you are." And by a codfish, he means the main culprit. The dog, marked out and shamed in this way, is supposed to keep the peace for a while at least.

The sea's covering of winter ice serves not only as a track for sledges but also as the stage for the hunting on which the region's livelihood depends. Even though Greenland's winter of 1912–13 was too mild up to the end of February, relatively speaking, it was still a good winter for catches, and very satisfactory for seals and white whales. Thus, there always was enough meat on hand. In one period of twenty-four hours, the hunters caught twenty-eight seals. Seal meat cost one ore the pound. You could eat any amount, since the price hardly mattered. But seal meat has a somewhat fishy taste, more than I had noticed in other marine mammals such as white whale or narwhal. Catches of shark, which are caught only for their livers, were also good. It might be of interest to give a more detailed account of the hunting of these voracious scavengers, which yield such good oil.

The dark line out there, one and half kilometres southeast of the station is a row of slaughtered sharks, the shark bank. To catch these gluttonous monsters, who are "thieving and cunning, known among all fish as insolent, beautiful, proud, and brazen," as an old book on natural history describes them, is so easy in the Arctic winter that even a child can do it. In a place about as wide as a house would cover are dozens of holes in the ice, a few paces apart, all with fishing lines hanging in them. To keep these holes from freezing up, they are frequently splashed with frozen tail fins or other pieces of sharks. The fishing lines are baited with snares, and other frozen slabs of shark serve to attach the part of the half-centimetre-thick line that is laid out on the ice. At first, it is hard to understand how a huge animal, two to four metres long, can be caught on such a relatively thin line, which looks as if it could be easily bitten through. And this would certainly be the case if a metal guard did not keep the shark from doing just that. The iron fishhook, almost a foot long and one centimetre thick, is attached to an iron strip with a cross bar or to a length of chain. The baited fish cannot bite through this guard, and thanks to the shark's buoyancy in the water, a thin line suffices when pulling the fish to the surface. To attract the fish when the shark bank is installed, tainted and pungent seal meat or a stomach full of rotting blood is lowered to where the sharks swim, fifty to eighty metres down. When the sharks take the scent and bite, then all one needs as bait are the gills or the stomach contents of a freshly caught shark. From time to time during the day, watchmen check the hooks to see if a fish has bitten. In that case, two men can easily pull it up. Enfeebled, with little resistance left, the uncouth beast emerges from the hole. While one man keeps pulling, the other lands a hook in the animal. With this, they can easily pull it out and drag it onto the ice. Although the people work with gloves, it is still cold work for the fingers. We once saw four sharks being caught within a short space of time. When pulled out onto the ice, the shark lashes to and fro with his tail fin, probably seeking to strike out, but his strength no longer suffices. His terrifying jaw with its pyramidal teeth is useless, because the fishhook is lodged there. A man or even just a boy now stands over the fish, and first cuts the baited hook out of the mouth, which lies far back from the snout. Then the brain and the long skein of the spinal cord are pulled out, rendering the shark as dead as a doornail. The fish has little blood but a lot of water in his body, which probably accounts for the rumbling sound that one hears when the animal is cut up. The brain and heart of a shark are amazingly small. In a fish that is two or two and a half metres long, the brain is only the size of a goose egg, while the heart of a four-metre shark is no larger than a child's fist. Cut out and flung down on the ice, it keeps beating slowly for quite a while – a strange sight. Even a dog will not immediately eat the pulsating heart of a shark. I observed one who repeatedly sniffed the heart, took it, put it down again, and finally decided to eat it.

In the stomachs of sharks, we found undigested hairballs and the moustache hair of seals, fat pieces of white whales – possibly bitten out of the live animal – and devil's fish. In contrast to the brain and heart, sharks' livers are remarkably large, almost as long as the fish itself. The man who harvests these has to lift his arms rather high in order to slip them into the leather collection bag. Even a small shark contains a kroner's worth of liver, considering that in Greenland money buys considerably more than at home. If the winter had only lasted a bit longer, Jost, who looked after a hole himself, might have ended up as a capitalist. Often a European and a Greenlander take equal shares in catching sharks. The former supplies the equipment and the latter the work. Like most important settlements, Godhavn has a station for rendering train oil to which, in the hunting season, shark livers were delivered on sleds and paid for by the hundredweight.

People disdain shark meat. I tasted it several times but did not develop a liking for it. It tastes sweetish and watery, amounting only to what I call half-meat. By contrast, the dogs are of a different opinion. They are part of the picture at the shark bank. For the dogs, this killing field is a magnet and a paradise, with its mutilated cadavers lying around stacked like cords of firewood.

Even harnessed to a sled, they will rush to attack the leftovers. After a while, however, they start to get choosy, and then they will not take just any old bite. Having eaten more than their fill at this banquet, they often end up in a sort of drunken stupor, from which they can recover only by sleeping it off. Just as Wagner's Siegfried brings a live bear to Mime at his forge, so young Thorbjörn Porsild – also a young Siegfried – once brought on his sledge from Jost's hole a whole shark that was still blinking its eyes, to be used as the station's dog food.

In January, fog banks hide the reborn sun. The snow on the white flanks of the Apostle and Lyngmarken fjords takes on a slight pink shimmer and the steep sides of the Skarvefjeld a warm reddish hue. The reflection of the sun! On the 18th, the sun actually appeared above the horizon for a short time. On 23 January, it was already light enough for us to restart observations with our pilot balloons. "What a different life this is," said Jost. "You almost feel it's spring."

But you seldom find someone who is really satisfied. Most people are not. Thus it was with the burgeoning light level. Enthusiasm for the bright nights is quite understandable and justified for tourists on a cruise to the North Cape or to Spitzbergen. A sunlit night has a special atmosphere, when the sea stretches like a mirror under a pale blue sky, and the icebergs stand solemnly, lit from the north. These beautiful pictures, however, lose some of their charm when repeated daily. The continuous light may be useful and indispensable in the tight schedule of an expedition, but it is a nuisance in daily life. If the "night life" in winter at the station did not always allow us enough time to sleep, then this was entirely a choice of personal lifestyle, whereas in the summer, when it is often impossible to sleep, you change, *nolens volens*, the night into day, reading and going for walks. So it could happen that, as early as mid-March, someone familiar with the midnight sun would exclaim "Here we go again with this confounded daylight." Yes, in Greenland, a country where you can never sleep your fill, you come to miss the beauty of a real summer evening, when dusk slowly fills up the bowl of night.

The Greenlanders are known to be witty and bright and always in the mood to lampoon you, as we ourselves found out. At first, I must have struck them with my height, 186 centimetres, but later it was Jost who astonished them with his strength. As an expression of astonishment – as we might say "holy smoke!" – it became the fashion in Godhavn to simply say "Stolberg" and later "Jost." A man like Jost, who could stash a seventy-five-kilogram hydrogen cylinder under each arm, was something else altogether. I wonder whether "Jost" was incorporated in a later edition of the Greenlandic dictionary, in the same way as the favourite expression of the Hutterite missionaries, "Ach, ja so" (Oh, really!), is preserved in the verb *ajasopok*, meaning, "to be astonished."

There is another saying that was making the rounds at our time among the Danish colonists, a Solomonic reply by the four-year-old daughter of a pastor. The mother told the child: "You are a silly little girl, you have no sense yet."

"But I have a harmonica," answered the child. This meaningful expression, "But she/he has a harmonica," is now conquering the area round Disko Bay.

As the sailors have legends that they swear to be true, so the views of even the converted Greenlanders are still interwoven with much superstition. A telling example is connected to the Arctic Station. The Greenlanders believe in shamans, the Angakoks. With their demonic arts, they can influence wind and weather and therefore the hunt, evoking a frisson of terror. Even after their death, these shamans can still raise mayhem by haunting the place. The Greenlanders call the site of the station Angakugsarfik, the Angakoks' place. The settlement of Europeans there, as long as they live at this particular spot, is an insurance against the witchcraft of the Angakoks and has been put to good use. In a crevice of the rocky ridge behind the station is a hidden Angakok skull, which Magister Porsild discovered when one of the dogs sheltered her litter there. The skull didn't get there on its own, of course, and inquiries traced it to a stone tomb, that of a shaman, situated between the station and the lagoon in front. Almost every day, the women and girls of the colony had to pass the place on their way to the other shore of the Rödelf where they often gathered kindling from the dwarf willows at the foot of the Skarvefjeld. They all agreed that they had been grossly harassed and annoyed for quite some time by bawling, growling, whistling, and other mischief when they were passing this gravesite. And so they refused to bring wood from the Skarvefjeld. But one needs wood, and it would harm the whole settlement if this was allowed to continue. So the community's very existence was threatened by the scandalous conduct of the skeleton in the stone pile, an outrage that could not be tolerated. But what could be done?

Two courageous hunters found the right solution. They stole the skull and hid it in the place described above. This brought peace, for a skeleton in Greenland can only go a-haunting when he has his skull with him, and when this was taken away, the Angakok, in a sense, lost his license – an elegant solution. This might also be a good idea in our land, where headless figures quite often put in an appearance. Now the station lies as an invincible foreign body between the skull and the bones and, as long as Magister Porsild lives at the station, the spell cannot be broken. This could be one more reason to incorporate the Arctic station as one of Denmark's public institutions.

The clock of world events had stood still for us. The latest European news that we had heard dated from July 1912. By now, it was March 1913 and the day approached when we were supposed to send out our own news by dog-sledge post via South Greenland. Although there was really not so much to say, a frenetic round of letter-writing started at the station and among the colony's Europeans. This sledge post, which starts in the northernmost colony of Upernivik and goes, if possible, as far as Holstensborg and the first departure of the *Hans Egede*, costs the Danish crown thousands. It is no easy task for the mail couriers. Just last winter the uncertain ice conditions forced them to make enormous detours. Over long stretches, the sea froze late and was partially broken up again by storms from the southwest. Between Ritenbenk and Jakobshavn, the sledges had to turn east via the Ata Sound as far as the inland ice sheet. A letter from Godhavn to Egedesminde took weeks. This is a direct distance of a little over sixty kilometres – the *Hans Egede* does it in four hours – but the necessary detour around Disko Bay stretches the journey at least sevenfold.

There were rumours that Knud Rasmussen, the Greenland man par excellence, and his friend Peter Freuchen were also on their way from Cape York to Holstensborg to meet the first steamer. The rumour proved true. These two daring men had accomplished the trip to Pearyland and the Danmark Fjord in 1912. Porsild received a letter from Knud Rasmussen himself. The mail and Rasmussen finally managed to reach Holstensborg.

By the end of winter, "When will the mail arrive?" naturally moves more and more to the forefront of the Europeans' minds. By April and May, the topic was foremost in all conversations. There were, of course, false alarms. On 9 May, someone claimed to have seen the longed-for mail kayak toward the south in the still drifting ice, but there was nothing in this.

The first day of Whitsuntide arrived. It was a wonderful morning, the snow walls around the house had disappeared, and so had the shark bank. Snow finches were twittering, and metallic glittering flies were buzzing. The sea, free of ice, roared to announce the coming of spring. We sat by the open window at Richard Jensen's, an assistant at the station, when Erling Porsild stuck his head through the window and announced the mail. Because of the previous false alarm, we were not quite convinced it was true. Palase Mortensen went out to ask some Greenlanders. Much faster than he had left, he returned with the words: "Posten er kommen!" This exploded Jensen's coffee party. We all ran out and saw three hunters just arrived from Kronprinsen Island with packages wrapped in leather. Our letters!

Now started our reading campaign. At long last we received confirmation, as we had expected, of the eastern party's success, eleven months after we'd parted from them on the ice cap. There was a letter written in pencil by de Quervain in Angmagssalik, and also a postcard by Fick and Gaule from Iceland. We had always believed that, with the kind of preparations and the qualifications of the "eastern boys" de Quervain, Fick, Gaule, and Hössli, they would successfully conclude their bold journey. What was already known to the world we learned only now. We were also very satisfied by the other news from home. We only learned the details of the troubles in the Orient from the newspapers that reached us weeks later. (The voluminous newspaper packages are not sent by the kayak mail.) Among our letters, there were several dated from July of the previous year; one for Jost was marked "Express." I wonder when this one would have arrived without this caution by the sender! For the time being, however, Jost had yet to see it, as he was still in the highlands of the island with Porsild and Thorbjorn. That the mail service had already had a certain influence on the Greenlanders, who had accepted some of the glossy European forms of politeness, was proved when a letter to our Greenlander Elisabeth at the station was addressed to "Herr Elisabeth."

On 23 May, we were wakened early in the morning with the shout "Umiarssuit, umiarssuit!" (A large ship, a large ship!) And there to the south, between a promontory and an iceberg, we really could make out a thickening in the fog. Through the telescope, the eye discerned tall masts. It was the motor schooner *Godthaab.* People can find each other in fog and ice, even in the Arctic solitude. Denmark's national flag, the Dannebrog, was hauled up the flagpoles, and cannons boomed out their greetings. We had been rediscovered! The *Godthaab* had to force an entry into "port," however, as ice still lay a foot thick there, allowing sledge traffic into June. On board ship, we could greet our former Captain Scoubye and First Mate Kjoller. The latter had taken de Quervain and his companions from Angmagssalik to Reykjavik the previous fall. We were also very happy to see master machinist Hoffmeyer's portly figure and the leaner one of his colleague Jelstrup again. *Godthaab* brought a new inspector to North Greenland in the person of Doctor of Law Lindow, accompanied by his charming young wife.

A few days later, the Kronprinsen islanders visited for several days in two umiaks and several kayaks, among them the kayak-paddling midwife mentioned earlier. They camped opposite the station with their skin tents and household goods to catch *angmagsettes* (capelin). These fish prefer the kind of sandy beaches that are found in the surroundings of Godhavn. A chance for picturesque pictures! Unfortunately, there was also a serious accident in June. It had to be pure killer instinct, because it could not be hunger at this time, when the eight dogs of a hunter from somewhere else attacked a four-year-old girl and mauled her throat. Although the wounds were immediately sutured (by strange coincidence the doctor from Jakobshavn arrived on his tour that very day after a nine-month absence) the poor child died a few hours later. This was the only death in the whole time since our arrival. The dogs were shot, of course.

The departure of the *Godthaab* was soon followed by the arrival of the *Eclipse*, the steamer that had taken the place of the *Fox* on the coastal route. Here we also found old acquaintances on board, including Captain Stocklund and his brother, the first mate. On 18 June, the *Hans Egede* steamed into harbour on her second visit. That was my cue to leave the stage of Greenland. Because of the very primitive and time-consuming process of loading and unloading, not helped by a strong foehn wind lasting several days, the *Hans Egede's* departure seemed to be delayed even further. The unexpected order to mobilize in the afternoon of the 25th therefore came very abruptly, just when Jost and I were working on a fair copy of the meteorological results. The ship's departure was imminent. Kifvak Elias appeared and wanted my hand luggage, which was not yet packed. The ship was already sounding its siren. By some miracle, I was packed in ten minutes, don't ask me how. We ran to the port. I had arrived here in night and fog and left the station like an absconding fraudster. My speech of farewell and thanks came with me to Europe, unspoken.

Dr Jost stayed behind. I had to leave him to face the imminent plague of mosquitoes alone. The observations that he and Magister Porsild had made on a two-week trip to Disko's unknown highland had to be completed, and Jost's participation in a circumnavigation of the whole island by motor boat, planned to complement the topographical survey, was of course desirable. In addition, he had an invitation from friends to Jakobshavn, reason enough for him to stay in Greenland to the end of August. A.P. Olsen, the previous acting inspector and his wife, Bestyrer Fencker and his wife and children, and the private teacher Moller-Pedersen also took the opportunity to leave Disko. They had all received us often during the long winter with warm Nordic hospitality, and it was a special pleasure for me to be with them a little longer.

On the return trip, there was still some pack ice and much fog in the Davis Strait. Sailing across the Atlantic Ocean, however, we enjoyed magnificent weather.

On 8 July we passed the Orkney Islands, and on 10 July the castle of Helsingör, *det store Späckhus* (the large fat house), as it is known, after a remark by a little Danish girl who had been born in Greenland and could not think of a more apt comparison when she saw the monumental building. As the day was far advanced, we stayed at the pier in Helsingör for the night. The Danes, who had been missing their forests, thought they could smell the wonderful beech groves of Seeland.

By the next morning, the last of the fur pants and anoraks had disappeared from the deck. Only Europeans were to be seen, wearing collars, some even with frock coats. The Fenckers had their Greenlandic nanny along. Now she, too, had to don a European-style dress. At first in her shame and embarrassment, the girl wouldn't venture on deck and crept into a corner near the stairs, holding her good Greenlandic fur pants in front of the indecent long dress, as if to protect her modesty. *Sancta simplicitas*!

Over the winter, I had been regaled with tales about polar bears that had appeared in Proven and Upernivik. Shortly before the reporters from the Copenhagen newspapers came on board, I recalled these stories. And this was only timely, as people who come back from Arctic trips should always be able to tell tall tales about their battles with polar bears!

ABOUT THE AUTHORS, TRANSLATORS, AND EDITORS

Alfred de Quervain (1879–1927) studied geophysics and meteorology at the University of Bern in Switzerland. After helping a noted French scientist discover the stratosphere, he joined the Swiss Central Meteorological Office as adjunct director in 1906. He visited Greenland in 1909 to conduct weather research and inspect the ice cap, returning in 1912 to make the first west-to-east crossing of Greenland, as described in this book.

Paul-Louis Mercanton (1876–1963) was appointed associate professor of physics and electricity at the University of Lausanne in 1904, where he later also taught meteorology and geophysics. During the Swiss 1912 expedition to Greenland, he led the so-called western party that stayed on the west coast to survey glaciers and collect weather data. From 1934, he headed the Swiss Central Meteorological Office in Zurich. Throughout his career, he published extensively on the variation of European glaciers.

August Stolberg (1864–1945) studied art history in Munich, Zurich, Bern, and Strassburg but also attended lectures in geography and geophysics. From 1900, he worked as a scientific assistant in the Alsace-Lorraine weather service, where he first met Alfred de Quervain. In 1909, he accompanied the Swiss meteorologist on his first visit to Greenland. In the 1912 expedition, he was a member of the western party, staying on through the winter to continue the expedition's weather observations.

Elisabeth de Quervain Schriever (b. 1919), the author's daughter, translated this book together with her husband, William Robert Schriever (1921–2018) in the early 1980s. Thirty or so years earlier, Bill Schriever's profession as a civil engineer and expert on the effects of snow loads on structures had brought them from their native Switzerland to Ottawa. As naturalized Canadian citizens, the Schrievers wanted their three children to know something of their grandfather's achievements in science and exploration.

Martin Lüthi is a glaciologist at the University of Zurich who has worked on Greenland's glaciers since the start of his career. He has contributed to exhibitions commemorating de Quervain's crossing of the Greenland ice sheet.

Andreas Vieli is a professor of physical geography at the University of Zurich. He has researched the dynamics of calving glaciers in the Arctic for more than two decades at locations that include the starting point of de Quervain's 1912 expedition.

Martin Hood works for an international organization in Switzerland and is a member of the Academic Alpine Club of Zurich. He is the translator of *One Hundred Mountains of Japan*, a collection of essays by the Japanese mountain writer Fukada Kyūya.

INDEX